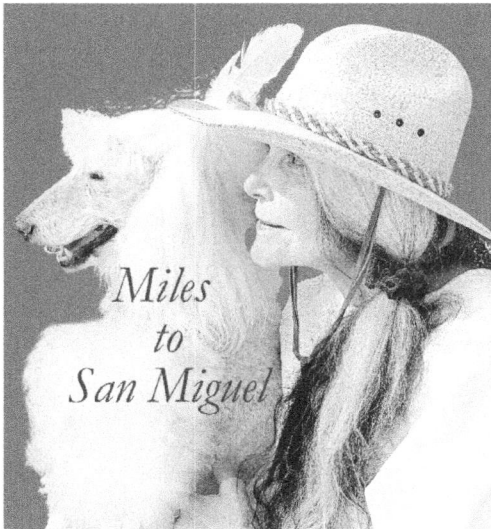

Miles
to
San Miguel

Miles

to

San Miguel

Lorraine Parish

San Miguel de Allende, Mexico

Contact information:

> Lorparish@aol.com
> Lorraineparishwriter.com

Mail:

> 4717 Valero Court
> pmb 0312
> Laredo, Texas 78046

This book is dedicated to the brave folks who have gone before me, and those who will follow, who have had the requisite courage and unwavering faith to take the leap to a new, uncharted life. And to the loyal customers over my forty-four-year fashion-design career — this book is for you.

Life should not be a journey to the grave with the intention of arriving safely in a pretty and well-preserved body, but rather to skid in broadside in a cloud of smoke, thoroughly used up, totally worn out, and loudly proclaiming, "Wow! What a Ride!"
~ Hunter S. Thompson

CONTENTS

Acknowledgments

I would like to thank Patricia Fogarty, the brilliant and generous editor I was fortunate to work with. I could not have written this book without her.

Also, a big thank-you to all the supportive friends who consoled me through the worst days, laughed with me on the best days, and always, without fail, cheered me on when I needed it the most — you know who you are.

And last but not least, thank you to Pearl the Magnificent, my fabulous poodle and wing-girl. You will live in my soul forever.

None of us have the promise of tomorrow. God forbid this is my last day on this beautiful earth, it won't be spent listening to some news person telling me how rotten we are, how rotten life is, heck no, I'm going out and seeing how beautiful life is. As humans, our time on this planet is very limited . . . Turn off, tune out, and turn on your life. Peace.

~ Frank Zappa

Prologue

Last Boat to the Future

The time for second thoughts, the time for mind-changing had come and gone. Behind, after one short boat ride, was a good life lived on Martha's Vineyard, one of the most exquisite places on earth. And ahead? The unknown.

I loved my home, the island I was leaving; she had loved me too. She nurtured me when I was young, gave me reassurance on my paths to success, failures, and unproven incarnations. But when my days there became too familiar to hold my interest, she gave me permission to go.

But it was I who detached from this magnificent place, not she from me.

Soon I will look through the rearview mirror on this vehicle that will carry me, my dog, and my trusty mannequin, Agatha (yes, I said mannequin) to our new home. And I wonder what my island will say to me as her image fades from sight?

Don't go? Go with my blessings? Come back soon?

Or, worse, nothing at all?

For comfort, I look to my right, where Pearl, my canine companion of twelve years, eagerly sits. I know then that our trip to this new place and the new chapter in our lives will be fine. She has no fears; she's with me, and for her, it is just another fun ride in a big, new, traveling machine.

And what are this regal animal's eyes eagerly focused on, down her long, beautiful white poodle snout? The clear, blue morning sky, of course, and nothing more.

This brilliant morning — the Universe's encouraging nod to our send-off — is, for me, a welcoming omen for a safe, if very long road ahead. And so I go, without a cloud in the sky nor a worry in Pearl's head as she turns to me and her warm eyes say, don't worry, Mama, and oh, don't forget the pee stops along the way. I laugh.

I so wish I could be her some days, especially today.

Yes, it's a glorious day for goodbyes, certainly too glorious for tears, unless they are ones of relief. Relief that the arduous physical work of dismantling a home, an iconic business, and forty-one years of an incredible life on this island is done. But, most important, it was done well. Besides, if the tears begin to fall now, they may never end.

And the ocean, his waters are a calm, crystal, marine-blue today.

My dear blue companion, it seems I have known you forever. Will I miss you? Will I see you again? I may not, so I say my goodbye. I know where you live if ocean-lust becomes too great for me.

I look to my left. To my surprise, a few friends are here to say their farewells too. In just moments, this profound life change has become more real, but still, no fears or regrets have clawed their way into my determined, laser-focused consciousness.

I can do this.

The sky, the ocean, my friends, my island, the Universe, Pearl — and even Agatha, riding shotgun — tell me so.

The twenty-eight hundred miles ahead of us is my life now. And for eight days, this trusty rental truck, shared with my menagerie in front and prized possessions in the back, will be our home.

The entertainment for these road-trip days will be the show outside our windows. But, as I will soon find out, the real show will be a cornucopia of memories coupled with my mind's imaginations. Luckily for me, the imagination show I've enjoyed for sixty-nine years is one not to be rivaled.

The boat is here, the ferryman waves his hand, and it is time for this truck to a new life to board. I tearlessly nod farewell to my friends and begin the overland journey to our destination — a beautiful, old, charming town in Mexico.

I take my cue from Pearl when she suddenly stands and happily barks, "Let's get going, and will there be chicken when we get there?"

I laugh again, put our home in drive, and take my last boat ride, but this time, it is the ferry ride to my future.

Chapter One

Adventure Rears Its Beautiful Head

September 2017

Unless one has lived through a serious illness or has been spiritually clobbered over the head for any of a multitude of reasons, we humans tend to trudge through life, day after day, year after year, until, if we are fortunate, the world stops spinning for a brief moment, and our past, our present, and, most of all, our future crystalize into one clear, powerful question that asks — *Now what?*

That very moment, that very thought, presented itself to me when I turned sixty-six. It was as if hundreds of quiet little intimations of discontent suddenly joined forces and became one big smack across the face. It said, "We're bored. Our days are numbered. We're dying here; this is not who we are."

I have always taken my own counsel. I trust my judgment and instincts, even though I have made many mistakes, and a few, to be honest, were considerable and life-changing. But it was I who made those choices, and being alone in the world, there was no one but myself to reap the rewards or pay the price. I survived those mistakes, and I grew from them. They were meant to be — were preordained, in a sense — and I say this with complete sincerity and without regrets.

So, suddenly, feeling restless after thirty-eight years of contentment in a place I loved dearly, I asked myself a life-altering question. It was the most serious of all the questions I had confronted in a very long time. And the answer, whatever it was to be, would have profound consequences for me.

"Lorraine, this could be your last chapter. Is this beautiful place, which has been home for so long, where you will choose to spend your final years?" An unexpected loud, firm voice resounded from my mouth; it came from a place within that I had yet to know, and it said — *No!*

Once again, I asked myself — *Alright, then, now what?*

What comes next after a defining moment like this? Should my response be, "Question, go back to where you came from. I can learn to live with boredom and the misery of knowing that each day could have been another day of adventure, had I not been so fearful."

I have never been a coward, so I was out of luck pretending that this big thing, this grand realization that I needed to move on, had never happened. I am a planner, which, as you know, makes God laugh. Therefore, I am one of God's, if you believe in God, favorite comedians. It was time, then, for one big final laugh — I mean plan.

"Hey, you, the God Who Laughs, are you listening? I'm going to sell everything and move to Mexico! Hilarious, right?"

I am a recovering alcoholic and therefore have taken deep dives into my thinking and beliefs. A self-examined life is the only life worth living — that is a philosophy I fervently subscribe to.

And since I believe in this philosophy and was closing in on seventy, I knew in my heart that I could not sweep this cacophonous awakening under the rug, and anyway, the worm of obsessive thinking was already twisting its way through my consciousness. It began the second the seed of change was planted, the second the question was asked and answered.

For years, I had heard about a beautiful, charming historic town in Mexico named San Miguel de Allende. Many of my friends had lived there in their youth or had visited the town recently. I thought, since the Universe keeps throwing that town's name out to me, why not start there in the search for a new life?

So I did.

November 2019

I left for an exploratory trip to San Miguel in November 2019. Those of us who have had our feet planted on planet Earth for the last several years know *that* date is a *before* date — before the pandemic of 2020.

It's funny — well, actually, it is not funny at all — but among the hundreds, if not thousands of logistical difficulties a pandemic can cause are complications to major life decisions.

Many of us were caught with our pants down, and unfortunate instances of bad timing — actions that might have been seen as courageous or brilliant in pre-pandemic days — became gigantic, unforeseen blunders.

I, the pragmatist — really any rational person — would need a serious reconnaissance trip before taking a plunge like the one I was considering. What's more, a reasonable person would follow up such a trip with a few years of on-and-off visits, but time was not on my side. And, I'll admit, I did a rush job and put my "gut instincts" decision maker into overdrive.

I went, I explored, I asked any English-speaking person I came across, especially those with dogs, a string of nosy questions. I was on a mission from my soon-to-be future life, and thankfully, shyness had been my adversary only when I was young.

Every day in San Miguel was another day to open myself up to my longtime friend, Intuition. She has been my number one adviser from the day I left my childhood home at eighteen. She had also guided me through other hair-raising, life-altering decisions, such as the one that inspired my move to the island at the age of twenty-eight.

And until November 2019, those kinds of moments in my life, as gut-wrenching and scary as they were, were nothing compared to the most significant life change I was contemplating. And by the time this transformation would be accomplished, I would be sixty-nine years of age.

Sure, I had my stable of lessons learned and experiences experienced. But because those extra forty-one years of wisdom were sprinkled with failures, I knew the risks. I knew what I would be giving up — a successful life in a place where I was loved (though surely disliked by many) and admired — and I knew with certainty that there were no guarantees of success and happiness waiting for me down the road in my not-so-distant future.

And this future would be in a foreign land, where I knew no one and no one knew me.

Fate has a way of intervening, though, and on my reconnaissance trip, it led me, by chance, to a kindred spirit, another fearless traveler in life — a younger soul-sister, you could say. And meeting this familiar woman, who shared her past while I was facing my possible future, changed my life forever.

Her name was Sharon, and this book is the story of our relationship before and during the pandemic of 2020 and the road journey of nearly three thousand miles it took to get back to her and beautiful San Miguel.

We must be willing to get rid of the life we've planned, so as to have the life that is waiting for us. The old skin has to be shed before the new one can come.
~ Joseph Campbell

Chapter Two

Sharon

I met Sharon on the third day of my exploratory trip to San Miquel. I was poking around one of the town's many antiques shops, looking for nothing, but hoping to find a treasure whose magic only I could see.

What I discovered was not a something, but a someone. And when I found her, I knew she was to be, and possibly always had been, significant in my life.

Fateful encounters like this are the ones we all dream of, and they are usually just that — dreams. But this was not a dream; this was real.

While admiring a beautiful, ornate gilded mirror, I caught the reflection of an eerily familiar young woman. I became fascinated with her when, suddenly, her dark eyes locked on mine. And to this day, I vividly remember those warm eyes in that gilded mirror and how they radiated a kind, gentle *knowing* as they invited me in.

I felt emotionally and spiritually connected to her, and as the world seemed to fall away, I sensed a trust radiating from her, the kind of trust I have only experienced with the amazing canines I have loved over the years.

Who was this fantastical person? A past-life encounter, a long-lost spiritual twin? Who cared? Living in *this* moment was the only thing that mattered to me. It soon became clear that our fates had merged; we were cut from the same cloth, with our differences measured only by years.

Sharon and I spent the following days — they sometimes seemed endless — exploring this incredible, goose-bump-producing town. The spell of the other worldliness we shared was enhanced even more so by the mystical-like atmosphere of San Miguel.

Each day, we sensed that our time in this extraordinary place was one less day we would have there. And as the days slipped by, we began to silently count the hours.

The day of our departure, of course, came, and when it did, Sharon and I simply said, "See you soon" — not to each other but to the charming town where we had spent many wondrous days. We knew we had more beautiful times ahead, so why spoil today with an emotional goodbye?

Off I flew, back to my world of discontent, knowing what lay ahead — the dismantling of a life I had loved but one I could no longer live.

Nothing is absolute. Everything changes, everything moves, everything revolves, everything flies and goes away.
~ Frida Kahlo

Chapter Three

The Unthinkable

Upon arriving back home and after my anxiously awaiting dogs had their way with me, the island realtors began calling. They knew of my, hopefully soon-to-be plan to move, and with house inventories being low, they were eager to know of my decision.

In early February 2020, a week before my house was put on the market, I became ill with the worst flu of my life. Rumor was, there was a virus going around the community that, on occasion, developed into pneumonia.

Sure enough, I landed in the hospital late one night with a fever and the beginnings of pneumonia. I was bedridden for days; a full recovery took weeks. And during that time, covid came on the scene.

In March 2020, the world was stunned. For me, the most alarming of all the unknowns was that not one person, it seemed — not doctors, world leaders, or even scientists — knew much of anything. There was no one at the time whom we could look to for guidance — *no one.*

I am not easily frightened, but I was definitely worried. Not just for my health but for my financial survival. I had flown by the seat of my pants since the crash of '08 and, to tell the truth, had been successfully scraping by for most of my professional life. During some years, my business had survived just from sheer will, and I was tired of the struggle — and now this.

Dear lord, how do we get through the days ahead, and most of all, what will we, as a nation and a world, look like on the other side?

One thing I was certain of, there was no way I was selling my home under these circumstances. There was not a snowball's chance in hell I was pulling the rug of security out from under me — leaving the companionship of my friends, the refuge of my house, the sanctuary of my little town — and moving to a foreign country.

No way.

Although my house was snapped up before I could make the decision to take it off the market, the sale fortunately fell through at the last minute.

Disheartened and scared before this good luck happened, I had bravely given my future to the Universe. And in the end, the Universe, of course, had my back, like it did when I sold the house again, a year later. This second time, though, like millions of houses all over the world, it sold more quickly and for a lot more money.

One of the many blessings I experienced during these months was the time I spent with my cherished standard poodle, Rudy. Because of his age and poor health, I had my doubts that he could make it to Mexico with me and his niece, Pearl.

The extra year or so we had in our home, the only home he had ever known, was a beautiful but heartbreaking time for the three of us. And for this I will be forever grateful.

My dogs and cats, in my cat days, were always the glue that held me together when I felt my life falling apart. On some days, they were my reason to get up, and on the worst days, they were my reason for living.

When I think of the days at the height of the pandemic, I will forever see the three of us — me, Rudy, and Pearl — squished in a little twin bed I had set up on the first floor since Rudy could no longer climb the stairs.

I will never forget those cold winter mornings in that bed, elbows mashed to my side, writing one of my screenplays on my laptop, waiting for that old house of ours to heat up. I would gladly relive those days, with no hesitation.

The times we share with our treasured animals are defining periods in our lives. When they must leave us, we mourn not only the loss of these remarkable beings, but the eras in our lives that they represented.

And when these beloved creatures are gone, we realize those precious, fleeting chapters in our lives — events we may fail to grasp, moment to moment, day to day — are also gone, never to return, though they are forever burned into our memories and, painfully, into our hearts.

It was unequivocally the best of times, and unquestionably the worst of times.

The preferred medicine for me in those days, categorically, were the stories and memories I shared with Sharon, whose heart remained in San Miguel.

Our relationship developed into one of confessional storytelling, and our exchanges became invaluable as we coped with the frightening pandemic.

We told of our past indiscretions with men, drinking, drugs, going to jail, and questionable business decisions. And no matter what the sometimes-embarrassing tales were about, we were a hundred percent honest in the telling of them.

I began to make notes and eventually detailed transcriptions of our favorite and most scandalous stories. In the subsequent chapters, I've not only written about my and Pearl's road trip to San Miguel, I've also included these memories and musings here and there when they surfaced in what I came to call my "road daydreams." The tales became the relief and distraction I needed to lessen the monotonous tedium of driving.

Knowing Sharon was with me in spirit reassured me about what I was doing; it inspired me as I faced the challenging and daunting task of uprooting my long and happy life on the island in exchange for a new, unknown life thousands of miles away.

My days during the pandemic became, as for many single people, one of solitude, which is my natural, preferred state. I walked my dogs on the wooded paths near my home; I sewed hundreds of covid masks; I designed clothes; I wrote essays and screenplays.

But what I did most obsessively was watch the news. Didn't we all? The media was filled with daily barrages of hateful politics and gobsmacking news of the pandemic.

All of which became more worrisome by the day, due to our idiotic human responses to one of the most serious and dire world events of our lifetime.

As I age, I am increasingly astounded by the moronic folly of the human species. While nature sings her glorious tune, mankind bombs the hell out of her — this awareness has become my later-in-life cross to bear.

Being the human I am, I cannot escape this sorrow, I can only endure it, write about it, and throw money at the good causes fighting it.

But maybe, just possibly, a life surrounded by a totality of newness can ease some of the sadness I feel and lessen the effects of the anger that I witness around me.

One can hope.

The thing that gave me the most pain in life, psychologically, and it gave me tremendous pain psychologically, is man's disrespect for nature.
~ Joni Mitchell

Chapter Four

Lollygagging on the Other Side

I was nearing the end of the boat ride and have not a clue as to where my thoughts wandered during the forty-five-minute trip to the mainland. Most likely, I kept my attention on the new Rand McNally road map I had recently bought — no Google Maps and rote computer voices for me, uh-uh, no thank you.

What I feel sure of, though, is that any ruminations I may have had never wandered into the negative. For more than a year, I had felt guided by positive energy, and this energy had but one request — unwavering faith.

My best friend, also a believer in such things, had seen its magic time after time and would remind me of its existence whenever I had the slightest doubt.

Even today, knowing that my life transformation turned out to be far more difficult and painful than I ever could have imagined, my faith in this energy has remained steadfast and strong.

The constant pattern of even the smallest act falling into place was extraordinary. And after all my years of living, nothing I had ever attempted had happened so easily and openly. So I held firm in this belief in providence every single day and every step of the way.

Once the ferry had pulled into the mainland harbor and we had driven off, I searched for a parking spot for our truck. My concern, I thought, was for Pearl and her well-being (the need to pee) on the nine-hour drive ahead of us.

This charming port, seven miles over the water from Martha's Vineyard, was nearly as familiar as my own hometown. In my forty-one years of waiting to catch the boat there, as I traveled back to my island home, how many hours had I spent wandering around this beautiful little village?

It was odd. I found myself in no rush; more accurately, I was completely unaware of time. I spent more than an hour aimlessly walking the harbor streets, pretending it was about Pearl doing her business before we hit the road. But if you knew my delicate Pearl, you would also know that was wishful thinking on my part.

When it occurred to me that I was actually saying more goodbyes and avoiding the long drive ahead, we headed back to the truck, where Agatha patiently waited. I then quickly got the show on the road before any sentimental thoughts could take hold and drag me down to a place of uncertainty.

There were no chances to take at this juncture of my herculean life transformation — *none*. There were eight days and nights ahead of us, with no room for error. Changes to my planned route due to weather were conceivable (and it did happen), but changes of heart or mind were not remotely in the realm of the possible.

After this little jaunt, no more lollygagging was allowed on our travel agenda, but making good time to Laredo, Texas, on the Mexican border, was. And after Laredo? Months prior, I'd hired a driver for the last leg of the journey to San Miguel de Allende, Mexico, where our next life chapter would begin.

This beginning included closing on a new home. I had managed to buy a charming Mexican casa from an international online real estate company during the pandemic. This house would be where we would spend weeks and months recovering not only from our trip, but for me, years of stress and worry. And I knew for certain I'd also be contemplating the unavoidable question:

Now, who the hell am I?

I had made hotel reservations with a dog-friendly chain along the route to Laredo. The first big push was nine hours if Pearl and I were to arrive at the first hotel before dark. I had not questioned whether I could drive this distance; I had had plenty of experience, years of long hours driving my company van up and down the eastern seaboard.

But that was quite a while ago. I was sure, though, that if my mind's attention held fast and stayed strong, I would have no problems getting us to our first destination.

I believed I had thought of everything, but never had I given any consideration to my rear end. Why would I? At sixty-nine, I was mostly concerned about my attention span, and rightly so. However, in the fifth hour of driving, I found myself fighting a moment-to-moment battle of mind over behind.

The mind won in the end, but only after my rear end became so numb it was completely, totally silenced. I got us to that night's lodging on time, and as I limped through the hotel's sliding glass doorway, I mumbled to myself to never again attempt a drive that long in one day. I kept that promise, and my backside was grateful for it.

Incredibly, though, during that first day's long drive, what my mind had become preoccupied with, apart from my agonizing behind, was the amazing thing that began to reveal itself during our third hour of driving. It was something I never could have anticipated or imagined. It was truly astonishing.

As strange and mysterious as this phenomenon was, it was far more wonderful than frightening. And in many ways and on many days, it continues to intrigue and haunt me.

The clearest way into the Universe is through a forest wilderness.
~ John Muir

Chapter Five

Bewitched But Not Bothered

The extraordinary event that slowly began to manifest in the first few hours of our road trip was, singularly, the most unusual experience of my life. But before I describe this peculiar phenomenon, I need to share my complete love and utter fascination with trees — all kinds of trees, although, of course, I have favorites.

I especially adore the sound, smell, and beauty of pine trees. These enchanting trees remind me of my childhood days on the Tennessee River — swimming, water skiing, then drying off under their canopy, the perfumed air heavy with their scent.

During the last twenty-five years of my island life, I had gravitated more to the wooded paths than the island's oceanfront and beaches. I began to find more peace and solace when I was deep in the woods, surrounded by trees.

For the many years I had traipsed about in the woods, I had had no knowledge that experiencing the flickering of sunlight between trees has effects similar to a healing method used to treat victims of post-traumatic stress.

So, unknowingly and for quite some time, I had been restoring my mind naturally in response to life's distresses and upsets.

I thought my only reason for this daily ritual "tree immersion" was for the tranquility I felt when enveloped by these incredible, stock-still beings. And they are beings to me. They are so goddamn alive, and it had taken me my entire life to become conscious of this remarkable truth.

Sometimes, while walking my dogs in the woods, I would find myself standing so still, it was as if I were in a trance. I just stood there, absorbing the trees' quiet energies. I also learned that this thing I was doing was a form of meditation and had a name — "forest bathing" — and that is exactly what it feels like, being physiologically bathed by trees. The peace and tranquility one feels while doing this simple act are extraordinarily calming.

In the years leading up to this ambitious move of mine, and possibly because I knew I'd be leaving at some point, I spent hours each day walking the island's trails, inclement weather be damned. The rawer the weather, sometimes the better; it was invigorating, and my canine companions could have cared less if we became cold, wet, and muddy.

In the winter, I'd leave food for my beloved deer and would actually be giddy the next day when it had disappeared. And it *was* the deer. I knew for certain by their little hoofprints in the soft, frozen, or snow-covered ground.

My days were never quite right if I did not walk among the trees, once in the morning and once in the evening. The trail I walked most often, especially during covid times, was so familiar that, after a while, I knew nearly every tree along the way by heart.

Spring, summer, winter, or fall — it didn't matter, I always recognized my favorites, no matter what they wore or did not wear. I knew them as well as I knew the familiar faces I would see shopping at the grocery store after our evening walks.

Yet I had not understood how much this tree passion of mine had seeped its way into my psyche until this drive through some of the most beautiful, tree-covered land in our country.

On this first day of leaving my former life, the immense rolling hills and mountains of the Northeast oddly seemed greener than usual. So much so, I could hardly keep my eyes on the road.

Then the most extraordinary thing began to happen. As I drove along the highway, the trees — the ones near the road and the ones as far as I could see — became much more than a lovely, green view out our windows.

They were becoming an obsession, and not just any run-of-the-mill obsession, but one of awe, curiosity, mystery, and love. It was a blend of awareness and emotion I had never known.

I'll just say it — it was as if they were beckoning me. I felt a strong, physical pull radiating from them, and the fact that this was actually happening was astonishing. This may sound irrational, but they were communicating with me. They were saying: pull off the road, walk into our forest, lie down among us, smell us, smell the earth, wrap yourself in our fallen leaves.

This phenomenon continued for days.

In the beginning, I thought their soundless voices and my urge to follow their call would simply fade, but it never did. On day three, though, I came very close to giving in; it had become a compulsion, and as a sober woman, I knew about compulsions and where they may lead.

Although I did not succumb, the fascination stayed with me all the way to Texas, where, as the trees lessened in numbers, so did their power.

This remarkable and welcome awareness had slowly become another companion and distraction for me on our long road journey to a new life.

I was never worried or concerned for myself, even though I knew what I was feeling was odd — very odd. But I was surprised that only now was I awakening to the fact that trees had become more a part of my being than I had realized. How could I have not known this?

Then I *knew* — it was the *trees* that I was going to miss the most. The part of Mexico where we were to live did have trees, but I had not felt a bond or connection to them when I'd visited two years earlier. They were not green, tall, and lush like the ones I had known all my life.

Even today, I can still feel their pull and hear their quiet voices whenever I watch a movie or see photos of rolling hills and forests.

I am convinced that this strange and beautiful gift, as I like to think of it, will never leave my consciousness. And I am grateful for it.

It wasn't very long after I had settled in to the rhythms of the road and accepted the haunting power of the trees that I began to allow daydreams to flit at the edges of my mind.

The most consuming daydreams were the ones of Sharon. We had both been brought up in the South, and our personal stories, even though we were years apart in age, were sometimes uncanny in their similarities.

So, with eyes glued to the road, and my driving confidence more secure, I let my mind wander back to the untroubled days when Sharon and I wandered the narrow, cobblestone streets of San Miguel.

But I truly became lost in thought when I recalled the entertaining, uncensored memories we shared with each other during the long, lingering, and worrisome days of the pandemic.

Trees are sanctuaries. Whoever knows how to speak to them, whoever knows how to listen to them, can learn the truth.
~ Hermann Hesse

Chapter Six

Next Stop, Harrisburg

My wing-girl Pearl had not a problem on the nine-hour drive to Harrisburg. She napped, she stood, she stretched, then napped again. The captain of the ship also had not a problem with her attention span, which was mostly due to the handy bag of chocolate-covered coffee beans in her driver's-side door pocket.

Weeks before I hit the road, I had decided on a different route than I usually took to Alabama, my home state and the midway mark to Laredo. In the past, on my long-distance clothing shows up and down the East Coast, I had always driven I-95. I had grown to passionately detest that stretch of highway so much that, for this trip, I took I-81. Unfortunately, I found it almost as congested with eighteen-wheelers as I-95.

Damn.

For thirteen years, during the Vineyard's off-season and needing money in those beautifully quiet but cash-strapped months, I did bimonthly trunk shows with my clothing line. I traveled up and down stressful I-95, driving as far south as Huntsville, Alabama, and Atlanta, Georgia, and as far north as Boston, Massachusetts, making stops in Greenwich, Connecticut, New York City, Philadelphia, Pennsylvania, and Washington, D.C., along the way.

In the early days, I had three or four employees working the shows with me. Those days were great fun and usually turned into major shopping sprees before we headed back to the island to regroup. We'd unload, count inventory, and resupply; then those of us who were single would hit the road again.

But as hard times fell, and they are cyclical, my employees dwindled down to one, then to none. The last five years of those events I did alone with my two fabulous poodles Noli and Cleo. These gorgeous creatures had become a big part of my trunk shows. In fact, over the years, customers sometimes came just to see them, and while I worked, they would take them for pee-pee-poo outings in Central Park or around the block of whatever four-star hotel I had set up shop in.

Years later, I occasionally asked myself how in the world did I do those nerve-racking, challenging shows; the physical work alone was massive. Not just the driving, but the setting up and breaking down seem near impossible for one human being to have done. Granted, I had a great deal of assistance from the bellmen at every hotel, but the answer to that question is simple: *youth*.

Still, I will forever be amazed at the strength and energy it took to do just one show, much less three or four in a row. It was drive, unload, set up, sell, break down, load, drive, unload, set up, sell, break down, load, drive, unload, set up, sell. And that is exactly what I did for years during the fall, winter, and spring months.

It had been twenty-one years since my last trunk show, and I had not been on any kind of road trip since. So it was understandable that reminiscing about those traveling show days, coupled with my New York garment center years, were the first memories that came to mind on this long drive to Mexico.

However, throughout this present-day road trip, all kinds of nostalgias popped up. Usually they sprang to mind out of nowhere; a few, though, were remembered simply because of the state we were traveling in. But most were just wonderful, random remembrances I found entertaining as the miles went on and on and on.

Along the way, I invented another form of amusement for myself: catching the thing that triggered my free-floating train of thought. We all do this; you begin with one thought, one memory, and within minutes, you're ten, twenty years into your past. It was a curious process — backtracking memories to see how my mind connected the dots from one life recollection to the next.

But I didn't just fantasize about my own personal narratives; many of my of road imaginations were of Sharon's wild and crazy past. We shared a few personal stories in San Miguel, but soon after I returned home, we ditched the regular chitchat and went straight to the sometimes endearing but mostly juicy, mortifying stuff.

Our no-holds-barred storytelling became so much fun for me, as I said earlier, that I began to make transcriptions of our best narratives. I wrote down these tête-à-têtes as much as possible in the way they were told, and whether they were naughty or charming, recalling them helped stave off the sometimes-grueling hours of driving. But, most of all, they helped quell any traitorous anxieties or possible regrets lurking around the perimeters of my overactive imagination.

Sharon's tales, due to her being the sailor-mouthed, wild, free, radical hippie that she was, tended to be about her dance career, drug taking, unsavory boyfriends, going to the pokey, and her sometimes reckless, although memorable New York City escapades.

My narratives, in contrast to hers, accurately portray me as the pragmatic, occasionally immoral businesswoman that I was in those ambitious, going-for-the-brass-ring days. Though my stories sometimes seemed unexciting and less sensational compared to Sharon's, they nevertheless were undeniably traumatic and extremely painful for me. Well, for that matter, they would have been distressing for any normal, sensitive person.

Now that I was on the road again in more than two decades, right out of the gate, the tale my wandering mind conjured up was from my business life thirty-five years ago. I have always referred to this embarrassing, though not regrettable saga as my Peter the Millionaire story.

It involves one of my more questionable ventures in New York City. However, as it turned out, this particular indiscretion actually saved my business in the end, and I was able to continue my well-earned and loved livelihood for another thirty-two years.

My story's leading man, Peter, was a bona-fide millionaire (before billionaires came along), but more than that, he was a philandering husband who thought I, his damsel in distress, was a desperate woman without a strong, determined will and mind of her own.

Ha!

Peter the Millionaire:
Lorraine's Tale of Compromise

I don't know who is worse, Sharon — you, the drug-taking hippie, or me, the businesswoman-whore who slept with her fabric salesmen for their cotton sateen.

Let's call it a draw, shall we? Unless, of course, we are both just warming up to a crescendo of stories of transgressions in our pasts; if so, I say, let's hold off and save the Worst Person Award for another time. Maybe the winner of our "legal irregularities challenge" gets an all-expenses-paid trip to the pokey of her choice.

Now that I don't care what you think of me, I'll tell you my Peter the Millionaire story; he was definitely my foray into big-time financial whoredom. He was my last "business John" — that is, if you don't count an occasional roll in the hay that went on for several years with my married lawyer, just in case I needed him.

Sharon, have you ever had a literal roll in the hay? If I did, I must have been drunk because I can't remember ever doing such a fun, fabulous thing.

So, I was in New York, staying downtown near the South Street Seaport at my old friends' apartment, which had become my go-to place in the city. There was a restaurant nearby where I liked to drink and hang out after running around the garment center all day.

I loved those days in the garment center — the racks of clothes being pushed around the streets, fabric and clothing showrooms crammed into buildings everywhere. Such good energy on those streets back then. It was vibrant and exciting, and now it's mostly gone, ruined by all the terrible recessions, especially the Great Recession, and, of course, the advent of the internet.

It was a particularly warm, sunny fall day in New York in the year 1988. I was sitting outside at that restaurant going through my notes and swatches for the day when a handsome, overweight man walked up to my table. He introduced himself as Peter, the owner of the restaurant, and asked if he could sit and talk with me. Since I was open and available to any handsome, rich New York man, I, of course, said yes.

Peter and I immediately hit it off. He and his chauffeur-driven Mercedes picked me up that night, and our affair began. He told me right away he was married, but being the "working girl" that I was, I didn't care, and frankly, I was impressed with the fact that he was telling me this up front; most married men do not.

At the time, Sharon, I needed serious help with my business — I was unquestionably teetering on the edge of bankruptcy. I still had three of my best employees, and I was not going to let it all crash and burn. So why look a possible gift horse in the mouth? I saw it as my angels and guides — which I believe in — plunking this man down in my path to possibly rescue me. He wanted me; I wanted his money — I mean his help. It was mutual, and we were adults.

After a few months of seeing each other in New York, he realized I was not the cosmopolitan, hoity-toity businesswoman he thought I was. He had been impressed by the way I dressed (my designs, of course) and by the four gorgeous catalogs featuring my clothing line that I had produced.

They were some of the most unique, beautiful clothing catalogs in the country at the time, all photographed on charming, picturesque Martha's Vineyard.

My work was timely and right on the money, but the catalogs turned out to be too expensive for a small company like mine. The little beauties produced a lot of press and whoopla, but designing, manufacturing, and distributing the product on a broad scale was way above what my fledgling company could finance and manage.

Peter the Millionaire could see this — and that bankruptcy was the only way out. However, my work was so outstanding that, prior to meeting Peter, four venture capital firms had approached me. Within weeks, though, they had sent letters of regret. This was a month before Black Monday, the stock market crash on October 19, 1987.

These firms saw it coming and were pulling out of as many retail deals and letters of intent as they could. At the time, my cute lawyer, Henry, whom I never slept with, damn it, said, "Lorraine, most everything in life comes down to two things, luck and timing." I agreed because, six months earlier, it would have been a go with any one of those four firms.

I was personally and professionally broke, so broke that my three loyal employees and I prayed that Peter was our shining, white knight sent from fashion heaven. After a spur-of-the-moment trip to my house on the island, he decided to help, but not in the way we were all hoping for. He loaned me $10,000 for bankruptcy lawyers in Boston and, naturally, sent the money directly to the law firm.

He was no dummy, but actually, in the end, he was, because I was a bigger no-dummy — I out-no-dummied him because he never got paid! I had offered him the title to my antique car, but he, the dummy, didn't take it.

Sharon, essentially, this man wanted me to forget my life and business on the island and move to New York and be his concubine. I said, as you might have, fuck you, but if you are willing to invest $450,000 (a huge amount of money at the time) to move my business to NYC, I will consider it.

I then wrote a very detailed business plan to go with the ask. And, as you can imagine, that proposal did not go over very well, which I never thought or, truthfully, hoped it would. That was my price for leaving my island life, and therefore it was the end of Peter, the married millionaire from New York City. I remember the last time we talked, he said, "I hope this doesn't affect our friendship." I said, "Of course, it does. Have a nice life, and say hello to your wife."

I wonder where he is today.

I did the bankruptcy, got on the other side of it, signed a licensing agreement with some not-so-sophisticated clothing factory owners on the mainland, opened up two new stores, and kept on going. I was able to keep all three employees and even added a few more to the crew.

This Southern girl was not going to go down in flames. And that I'll-show-them Alabama-cracker chip on my shoulder I've told you about, well, it worked overtime for the next three decades.

A wise girl knows her limits; a smart girl knows that she has none.
~ Marilyn Monroe

Chapter Seven

Good Morning, Pennsylvania!

I am a fortunate woman in many ways. One is that I have never had trouble sleeping, whether in my own bed, someone else's bed, or a hotel bed; it doesn't seem to matter. And in a pinch, with no trouble at all, I have even been known to sleep on the floor.

This was to be my second day of traveling. I awoke refreshed, rested, with a good frame of mind, still free of fears or regrets. For weeks before I left my home and every day on the road, I consciously monitored my level of confidence or lack of it. I was never surprised by my positivity, for I had thought long and hard about the risks I was taking.

During the two years it took to bring this life-altering decision to fruition, I had had many conversations with myself. The exchange that seemed to give me the most strength was the one that went like this: *Lorraine, what if, once you get to Mexico, you regret pulling the proverbial rug out from under your life?* My answer was always a resounding, *Well, I will just have to fix it then, won't I?*

But the truth of the matter, which always sprang up in this same conversation with myself, was: *remember, by the time you get moved in and set up in your new home, you'll be seventy years old.*

That stark fact startled me every time I thought about my age, because, physically, I still felt pretty good, and until I looked in the mirror, I tended to forget how old I was. Even today, I continue this way of thinking, though with crossed fingers concerning the physical part.

Knowing time was not on my side — or anyone's, for that matter — I had kept focused on the prize in front of me and allowed nothing (except the pandemic) to get in the way.

And speaking of time, while driving the seven hours to our next hotel in Knoxville, Tennessee, I again amused myself by thinking of another anecdote I had shared with Sharon. This one concerned aging and why I thought the concept of "old" was not necessarily a bad thing.

But perhaps the more humorous thoughts I had, during the sometimes-arduous hours of driving, pertained to one of our storytelling threads — the subject of Sharon's unbelievably foul language. Eventually, I realized the undertaking was hopeless and so, sadly, gave up.

The idea of giving up reminds me of a little metal button a friend gave me eons ago. It said, "Now that I've given up all hope, I feel much better," and depending on the occasion, I agree, because it *can* be a good thing.

Sometimes one has to give up in order to let go and move on.

Lorraine's Philosophy on Aging

Sharon, I am curious, did your mother ever relinquish the impossible task of changing your disgusting speaking habits? No? Well, this is where your mom and I part ways. I'm not going to waste one more day or one more hour trying to change you. I love you just the way you are. (I hated that song.)

You and I have touched on our age difference many times, but I can see no relevance to it as far as our similarities are concerned. Nevertheless, since I am the older and wiser one, I will now share my views on aging with you.

A few years ago, an acquaintance said that, for her, turning sixty was hard to process because it had always seemed so far away, and this rang true for me. I also thought that aging is kind of like an unexpected knock on the door. You answer it, and on the other side of the door is you, and you're old. Given the opportunity, when that knock inevitably comes again, it would be nice to say, "Hey, old lady, get lost, you're too early. Why don't you come back, say, in a couple of hundred years, when I'm really tired and thoroughly fed up with living."

And so, Sharon, whenever I get the chance to defend the concept of aging, I like to say there's nothing wrong with things being old: old houses are beautiful, old cars are cool, old paintings are valuable, old furniture can be exquisite, old trees are the best, old dogs you love more, old architecture is genuinely impressive, and old people who have been paying attention in life are truly fascinating.

But you know what is not appealing when old? Food. You do not want old food. So, aside from food, old is good. Well, the exception could be old, moldy cheese, although that's a food I have no interest in; I'm allergic to it.

So, dear amiga, that is my philosophy on aging, though it could change at any moment, depending on how this ole body of mine feels when it gets up and gets going in the morning.

Covid still rages, but I hear vaccines are on the horizon. Wouldn't it be wonderful to have a vaccine shot in my arm before moving to Mexico?

And, please, keep encouraging me with my big move. Remember, it was you who inspired this hopefully wonderful thing.

"Age" is the acceptance of a term of years.
But maturity is the glory of years.
~ Martha Graham

I continued to keep my driving attention on high alert, even though I found myself on many occasions suppressing tears when, suddenly, out of nowhere, the memory of my amazing standard poodle Rudy, who had gone to the Rainbow Bridge before we left, would come to mind.

But, fortunately more often, I found myself bursting out in laughter over one of the many outrageous stories Sharon had revealed to me regarding her sometimes-scandalous past.

Both — tears and laughter — were good and were undoubtedly necessary.

Memories are a funny thing.

Every man's memory is his private literature.
~ Aldous Huxley

Chapter Eight

Road Confessions

With miles to go before our next stop in Knoxville, and my behind already killing me, I became worried whether I could endure another four hours of driving.

I had thought seven hours would be doable, but now my entire right leg had also become a problem. Counting the miles and anxiously watching the road signs as we got closer to the exit for our hotel became my main focus.

It's not easy for me to admit this, but my body was seriously feeling its age. And since my amazing road companion, Pearl, needed a pee stop and our stoic passenger, Agatha, whom I now called Her Ramrodness, could use a hat adjustment, I began looking for a place to gas up and stretch my aching legs.

When deciding that Agatha, the mannequin, should ride up front with us, it had never occurred to me that she would become our faithful sentry at night. All night and every night, she sat in the truck's cab, silently guarding our prized possessions in the back.

She had no need for coffee or pee breaks, but, most important, she looked as real as real could be — unless, of course, someone walked up to the truck's passenger window to talk to her; then the jig would be up.

Looking back, I wonder if this ever happened while Pearl and I snoozed away in our comfy hotel bed? It certainly could have, and I would have been none the wiser.

Due to the total silence from Agatha's side of the front seat, there were occasions when, out of the corner of my eye, I would catch a glimpse of a human form, do a quick double take, and think, what the fuck? These off-guard moments always made me laugh. Another confession: they happened quite frequently.

Several weeks before our trip began, covid had once again reared its ugly, frightening head. Nevertheless, I was committed to getting my future going, pandemic be damned. I had delayed my new life for two years, had had both vaccines, so why wait? Throughout those two years, Sharon and I had grown significantly closer and were ready to begin our life in Mexico.

Covid-wise, Alabama, my destination for a three-night layover, was in really bad shape; in fact, it was dangerous to be stopping there even for a day. At that time, my home state was the worst in the nation for the new Delta strain.

And because of covid, I have another confession to make: during the entire trip to Laredo, after filling up at big gas and convenience stops, I'd pull the truck to an isolated area of the parking lot, open the driver's door, sit on the running board, drop my drawers, and pee.

I had decided to do this even before I began my trip. I was still fearful of getting the virus, and the states that were ahead of me were not the biggest fans of masks.

To my way of thinking, why expose (pun intended) myself to a crowd of strangers at these pit stops — the fewer risks taken, the better.

I'd laugh for miles down the road every time I did this. I also happily confess that, for thrills, I secretly hoped a fellow traveler would catch me in the act.

A little thrill did occur one morning down South. Desperate for gas, I pulled into a questionable, godforsaken-looking roadside service station. The man working at this dilapidated old place actually nodded to Agatha as we drove in. He then flirtatiously said hi to her, but to his credit, he very quickly realized Agatha wasn't human and burst out laughing.

We both got a kick out of this hilarious and totally out-of-the-ordinary moment. I then decided to spare the poor fellow one of my pee performances; he had already had enough unusualness for the day.

Seriously, though, getting sick on the road would have been no laughing matter; it would have caused the ultimate setback, missing the closing on my new home in Mexico. Other arrangements could have been made, I suppose, but I had a timeline and did not want to deviate from it.

Again in the hope of avoiding covid, along with my where-to-pee idea, I had the ill-conceived notion of finding a safe place to park each night; I would sleep in the truck and not stay in hotels until Alabama. I ran this idea by a friend, who reluctantly told me that Walmart stores allowed overnight parking for big trucks and RVs.

Peeing in parking lots is one thing, but this ludicrous thought of overnighting in the truck was luckily squashed before I left the Vineyard. This reckoning was mainly due to remembering one of Sharon's more colorful stories of being arrested while sleeping in her van in Laguna, California.

In this rather harrowing tale, she described living in a little Econoline van in California while pursuing her dream of becoming a dancer. And, unbelievably, she did this living-in-a-car business smack-dab in the middle of Los Angeles.

Her story came to mind mainly for the reason that I was going into rather scary territory, where sheriffs and good ole boys ruled. And since I had decided, months prior, that covid was a preferable adversary to risks taken in unknown locations, I kept the truck pointed to the next safe home-away-from-home hotel.

Sharon's Drug-Bust Jail Tale

Lorraine, you asked for one of my being arrested stories. Well, here's one, and it was, by far, the scariest.

It's interesting to me that I had not one bit of shame. I was a young, adventurous hippie, living out my fantasy life, albeit one lived in a tiny home on wheels of a type that was wildly popular with us long-hairs back in the day.

These camper vans were not, of course, remotely like the chic, environmentally fashionable tiny homes of today, nor were we grungy little inhabitants of said homes like the modern-day trendy people living in their cool, itty-bitty houses.

Just so you know, my amiga, I'm committed to remaining in the spirit of our warts-and-all tales of confession, and so, here is my first tale of going to jail. It took a long time to arrive at an acceptable ending — not a happy ending, like the arresting cop losing his job, but one I could live with.

Though I had become a wild, flaming hippie in Manhattan, I was still seriously pursuing my professional dancing dreams. After a year, though, I decided that Manhattan life was no longer for me. My thoughts had nothing to do with the dance world; it was because I believed the best and coolest hippies lived in California.

So, moi, the wild-haired freak, preceded to drive her spiffy, used, white 1967 Econoline sleeper van across the country to California — land of hippies, spiritual weirdos, movie stars, dance opportunities, and common-variety loony tunes.

I drove the Manhattan-to-Albuquerque leg with Sheila, a fellow free spirit from New York who had friends living in New Mexico. She decided to stay in Albuquerque, and, sadly, this was the last time I would see her; she died a year later in a car accident.

I continued on to California with a high school chum we had picked up as we drove through my old hometown down South.

My high school girlfriend and I drove north from New Mexico to Colorado, then across Utah, eventually arriving safe and sound in San Francisco. We then drove down the amazing California coast to Los Angeles, and after a few days in L.A., unfortunately, she flew back home.

Now I was alone, living in my car, in an enormous, strange city where I knew no one. But, honestly, Lorraine, I don't remember ever being concerned or scared for myself.

It was an exciting, new adventure, and that eclipsed any fears I might have had. Now, though, looking back, maybe I was just too fucking dumb to see the dangers.

Dumb or not, I would pick neighborhoods that seemed safe for spending the night, but, really, what the hell did I know? The most important criteria for my little movable home was that the neighborhood have a service station nearby. The significance of this was that they had bathrooms, where I would wash my hair, take sponge baths, and do my morning business.

Surprisingly, I thought nothing of this. I was free and had escaped the small but wonderful, one-horse town I'd grown up in. Plus, I had had a year of the Big Apple experience, which included surviving many days of traipsing around the East Village out of my mind on LSD.

What could possibly happen to me in L.A. that I couldn't handle? Plenty, I am sure. Yep, my being dumb is looking pretty goddamn likely, isn't it?

So, there I was, living in Los Angles, juggling my dance aspirations alongside my more predominant penchant for hanging out with the cool California hippies.

By the way, my famous New York jazz dance instructor, Luigi, was initially upset with my California move; however, he agreed that it could be a good thing, but only if I went to Los Angeles and studied with his protégé, Hamma, which I did.

I had originally wanted to go to San Francisco, but Luigi was firmly against that. He said, "Sharon, if you want to continue to be a serious dancer — and you should — Los Angeles is the only place to be."

At the time, I believed — and so did many other struggling Hollywood wannabes — that sleeping in one's car was what any dedicated dancer, singer, writer, or actor would do until they made it big. And within a few weeks of arriving in L.A. in my rolling home, I discovered the beach town of Laguna, the location of my near demise.

A few days after discovering Laguna, I met a cute fellow hippie and happily began shacking up with him on weekends in his shitty, one-room apartment.

This became my routine: during the week, dance classes and looking for a waitress or a dancing gig; then, on weekends, driving down to Laguna and seeing my cute boyfriend.

One Friday night, I got to Laguna late. I was pissed off with him — why, I don't remember — but I had decided to teach him a lesson and not go to his place.

So I parked on a random street in town to spend the night. It was foolish and, as it turned out, illegal and definitely regrettable.

Lorraine, I had no idea that sleeping in a vehicle of any kind was illegal in Laguna — or anywhere, for that matter.

But that was merely a minor law I broke that unfortunate night. The scary and absolute worst law I broke, and went to jail for, was the possession of drugs — fucking drugs I didn't know I even fucking had!

While traveling across country, my girlfriend and I would occasionally pick up male hippie hitchhikers. It was fun. One of these hitchhikers had had a bag of tiny, white mescaline tablets. After a few "trips," I became convinced the pills were merely saccharine, not hallucinogens, but we all got high anyway, just thinking they were.

The Orange County cop found the bag of white pills in, of all places, the glove compartment — the fucking glove compartment — and I had been looking for that bag for days, too. Not only that, my hippie pipe belt buckle had marijuana residue in it. My living free as a bird came to a screeching halt that night, and I was all alone, thousands of miles from anyone whom I knew or who cared about me.

My boyfriend had no money, no phone, and he wouldn't have been of any help anyway, so I was truly alone in my terrifying dilemma.

I was in the Orange County jail for three demoralizing days. I can still hear the gulls calling outside my sad, tiny, barred window. I don't remember crying, but I do remember sleeping a lot.

Finally, a nice matron came by and said, "Honey, you've got to do something. Here's the numbers of two lawyers who can help you. And you have got to call someone to let them know where you are."

I bit the bullet and called my mother. I told her my situation, and, unbelievably, she said — these are her exact words — "How much money do you need, and where do I send it? And if you don't find a job and a real place to live, you are coming back home and going to college."

It was the going back home part that put a fire under me. There was no goddamn way I was ever going to do that. I was over eighteen and legally didn't have to do anything of the sort, but I loved my mother and needed her moral and financial support.

I got out of jail and drove back to L.A., now desperate to find a job and a place to live, which I did in a matter of days. Lorraine, isn't it funny how, at the age of twenty, the threat of moving back to your parents' home can be the impetus to quickly get your shit together?

I had big dreams and sincere aspirations to be a great dancer, and nothing was going to get in my way, except possibly myself.

I also went back to Los Angeles with my very own trial date. My memories of the legal logistics are fuzzy, but I distinctly remember that the two lawyers I had hired were concerned because the judge assigned to my case had a granddaughter who had died from LSD.

What fucking rotten luck, but the lawyers promised they were going to keep continuing my case until they could get a different judge.

One day, completely out of the blue, I got a call from them, and naturally, I thought they finally had gotten another less prejudicial judge. Two dear and loyal friends from Los Angeles suggested they go down to Laguna with me and hold my hand while I faced the music. And this was not Joni Mitchell music I was facing; this was the worst Lawrence Welk–Tony Orlando and Dawn kind of music, and I knew it.

The most frightening thing happened on the day of the trial. For the entire past year, my lawyers had said I had nothing to worry about. But when my friends and I were walking down the hallway toward the assigned courtroom, I saw my lawyers make a serious beeline toward me.

Fear was written on their faces. One said, "Are you prepared to go to prison today?" I literally went white and nearly fainted right there in the hallway. What the fuck had gone wrong?

As hard as they had tried, my lawyers could not get a different judge. It was a clear-cut case of an illegal search and seizure. Everyone knew it, but no one, I thought, gave a rat's ass about that except me.

Strange, though, during the trial, while the prosecutor and my lawyers were doing their thing, I was silently criticizing and picking them apart.

Even the judge and the policemen in that room were fair game for my silent critiquing. This mental act seemed familiar to me. Then I remembered — *The Stranger*, by Albert Camus.

The book's protagonist is on trial for murder, and he finds himself doing the same thing — mentally disparaging the jury members one by one. When he realizes what he is doing, he is baffled by this silent ridicule and his harsh judgments of the very people who have his life in their hands.

Needless to say, I was deeply fucking relieved when the judge saw the corruption of the arresting officer and ruled in my favor. Plus I looked pretty cute and remorseful that day.

Stay safe, my friend. You and I have a new, long, and lovely chapter to write in the not-so-distant future. Your Vineyard chapter is ending, and it is sad, but there is a bright new future waiting for you in Mexico.

Never forget, the lady in the mirror you met in San Miguel is rooting for you. You can do this, Lorraine. Don't ever have doubts.

Lorraine's Long-Ago
Embarrassing Sleeping Arrangement

Sharon, that was an intriguing but terrifying tale you told. To be all of twenty, just beginning your life, and staring down the threat of going to prison — well, let's just say that was a close call to a whole different kind of future, to say the least.

And I feel sure that, because of this experience, you immediately stopped your drug use, changed yourself into a fine, upstanding, and straight-as-an-arrow young lady who never again used profanities like the word "fuck"!

As I was reading your story about living in your car and rationalizing it as what you did for your love of dance, I remembered my own sacrificial living conditions when I was young.

It went on for several summers, and to make this reality acceptable in my mind, I convinced myself that what I was doing was simply dedication to my work. But more than that, I believed it would make fabulous copy for my biography one day — if I ever became famous, that is. Seriously. I am convinced we are the authors of our lives, and if I'm wrong, what's the harm in it?

I had left my husband (finally) in Manhattan, moved myself, my cats, and my business lock, stock, and barrel to the amazing island of Martha's Vineyard off the coast of Massachusetts. I knew no one on the island except an eccentric real estate agent I had befriended a few months earlier when vacationing there alone.

Sharon, and with your encouragement, this is what I am about to do again. But this time, it's a later-in-life, more dramatic, and riskier move compared to those days when I was all of twenty-eight and the world seemed to be my oyster. I felt I did not have much to lose, even though, looking back, I sure the hell did.

Since I kept finding myself broke after the first few summer-tourist seasons and unable to buy the quality fabric my designs were known for, it became clear I was paying entirely too much rent for my summer rentals, even though the places I chose were just simple little cottages.

I recall being angry with myself for jeopardizing the health of my fledgling business so early on in my transition to a new life. And so I made the decision — there is no other way to say this — to punish myself for being so irresponsible.

As a result, for the next two summers, the tacky commercial year-round space where we made most of my store's inventory became my summer digs. I slept under my cutting table on a cold, hard concrete floor for a period of four months each year until the seasonal rents went down in late fall.

My friends knew what I was doing, and either they understood and said nothing or were horrified and just looked the other way. I was devoted to my career in fashion design and had had moderate success in Manhattan.

Now, single and without a husband dragging me down with his insecurities and secret wishes for my failure, I had more reasons to succeed and prove my talents than ever before.

My two devoted employees showed up every morning at my workroom, aka my bedroom, and together we sewed the most charming clothes you've ever seen.

I had started to notice that my clothing line was beginning to reflect the gentleness of the island more and more each season. Although the dresses, blouses, jackets, and other garments could be worn in New York — or anywhere, for that matter — they had taken on a playful, soft quality that I now know was due to my new life and the peace I had found.

And if I had to sleep under my cutting table in order have the money I needed for good fabric, so be it.

You are going to appreciate this tidbit, Sharon. An absolutely adorable young man had a terrible crush on me and was more than willing to crawl under my table and "sleep" with me, any night I'd let him.

Barreling down the highway and getting closer to our dog-friendly hotel, I came out of the imaginative state of recalling Sharon's shocking going-to-the-pokey story and was surprised by how many miles I had driven.

I also realized I needed to pull my head out of the clouds and pay close attention to the road and the signs ahead. The last thing I wanted was to miss my exit and have to double back. My butt and leg would punish me even more if I let that happen.

As adults we try to relax from the never-ending quest for reason and order by drinking a little whiskey or smoking whatever works for us, but the wisdom isn't in the whiskey or the smoke. The wisdom is in the moments when the madness slips away and we remember the basics.
~ Willie Nelson

Chapter Nine

Night in Knoxville

With four more exits to the safe haven of our hotel and its comfortable queen bed, Pearl and I were becoming antsy and somewhat road weary. This was to be our second night on the road away from our former home, and interestingly, I had not found myself missing my old bedroom or its bed in the least.

Surprisingly, I had divorced myself from any sentimental feelings for my Vineyard house the moment we docked on the mainland. The truck had truly become our home in a matter of hours, and the one left behind had become a perfect example of how out of sight, out of mind can be a good thing. I was abundantly aware, though, that this was a necessary case of self-preservation thinking on my part.

However, before we left the Vineyard, a funny thing did happen concerning my bed.

Along with selling the bulk of my two stores' inventory, which was considerable, I was also shedding personal possessions (especially political books) I no longer needed or wanted.

My new home in Mexico came with beautiful furnishings: couches, tables, lamps, gorgeous built-in furniture, and a magnificent black-iron, four-poster bed.

I did not want an extra bed for this new home, so I needed to sell the bed I was sleeping in. I soon noticed that the act of doing away with this once-prized possession had begun to adversely affect my sleep, but not for the reasons you might think.

I'd wake up in the early, dark morning hours and think, damn, at some point, I have to get rid of this bed, and because of these thoughts, I could not fall back to sleep.

As I've said, I have never had trouble sleeping, but this looming, inescapable fact hanging over my head had become a considerable source of my exhaustion every day.

Therefore, I did what any rational person would do — I sold our bed right out from under us! And for the two months we had left living in that house, Pearl and I slept on blankets piled two inches high on the bedroom floor. They were uninterrupted, worry-free nights, though, and the much-needed sleep was, without question, worth it.

About this time in our downsizing, our incredible, beloved Rudy passed and went to the Rainbow Bridge. I still cannot bear to remember the last days of his life, at least just yet. And for the rest of the months Pearl and I lived on the island, I tried to keep my sadness under control.

Some days, I would become too downhearted and could not focus on the tasks at hand, so I found a place in my heart and put my gentle, little clown dog there and kept my love for him silently burning day and night.

And in this moment, as I write these words, not having Rudy with us for our new life in Mexico has been my only sorrow. He was as much a part of my and Pearl's existence as the air we breathed.

However, since we have left the house where Pearl and Rudy grew from puppies to old dogs, my darling Pearl has become happier by the day. Her attention during the entire trip road trip was focused on the highway ahead, where everything was new and exciting for her.

This morning, the second day of our road trip to Mexico, we had a potentially dangerous and undeniably scary experience. A car of three rough-looking men drove past us, signaling to the side of the truck. They had very worried, anxious expressions on their faces and kept pointing down at the tire (I thought) and gesturing for me to pull over.

The men continued doing this for ten miles or so. I did not hear or feel a flat tire, and from my large side mirror, I could see nothing wrong, so my immediate thought was that they wanted me to think I had a problem and pull off the highway.

I had heard similar stories of roadway danger and knew better than to put myself in such a vulnerable situation. I had brought along a few cylinders of mace and had them handy in case I had a threatening encounter and needed to defend myself. Concerned and somewhat nervous, I kept my attention straight ahead and made no further eye contact with the men.

At the time, there were no other vehicles on the highway, so another fear was that they would force me off the road. With this in mind, I sped up and kept the truck moving along at a good clip.

My vehicle was twice the size of theirs, and as far as they were concerned, there were two of us in the truck. Meaning me and Agatha. But then again, Pearl has been mistaken many times in a car for a human because of her head of hair; therefore, it was possible they saw three women — one for each of them.

Oh my, what a surprise it would have been for them to discover that their helpless female prey were not three hot chicks, but one old lady, a dog, and a mannequin! As worried as I was, I couldn't help but laugh at that ridiculous scenario.

Fortunately, since the exit for our hotel was not too far down the road, I began to feel safer and safer the more miles we put between us and the suspicious men in the car.

Once off the exit, I parked in the hotel lot, but before I went inside to check in, I anxiously looked for the possible problem on the driver's side of the truck.

When I found the source of their finger pointing and fretful looks, I laughed hysterically at what the mean, scary men were attempting to warn me about — the damn gas cap was dangling down the side of the truck. I had put gas in the tank, paid at the pump, and was so eager to get back on the road, I neglected to screw the cap back on.

Thankfully, it was on a chain. Obviously, I was not the only truck renter who had done this dumb thing, which prompted the rental company into, wisely, securing their gas caps on chains.

A week before I left the island, a good friend had overnighted a Saint Christopher (patron saint of travelers) medal to me. Before sending the medal, she had had it blessed by her priest, and I felt sure its divine woo-woo had silently been at work during my gas-cap escapade. And for all I knew, possibly, so far, our entire trip.

We checked into our comfortable Knoxville hotel room, and while Pearl ate her chicken dinner, I read emails from friends who were following us on our trip. Sharon and I were not to have communication until we met again in San Miguel. The reasons for this I'll save for later.

I closed my laptop after an hour or so. I was tired but knew I needed to eat — anything would do. Then a hot shower and hopefully a good night's sleep was to be had.

Agatha was outside guarding the fort, Pearl's ears, as usual, were on high alert, and the captain of the ship navigating us to our future in San Miguel was suddenly and gratefully going down for the count.

Never turn your back on fear. It should always be in front of you, like a thing that might have to be killed.
~ Hunter S. Thompson

Chapter Ten

Home, Sweet Home, Alabama

With only a short distance to our next hotel and being in no hurry, we hit the road late morning. An hour into the drive, as we drew nearer to my home state of Alabama — the state where I took my first breath, the one that gave me the foundation for a good life (yes, Alabama) and, in many ways, made me who I am — memories began flooding into my consciousness.

They were warm, soft-around-the-edges memories, so I welcomed them into my new road-warrior world of no responsibilities apart from getting Pearl and me safely from one destination to the next.

Since leaving my hometown at the age of eighteen, the moments of nostalgia that have surfaced the most are the ones of my family's cabin on the Alabama stretch of the Tennessee River.

In the months the global pandemic was raging, to help calm and quiet the anxieties caused by covid, Sharon and I shared memories of our safe, beautiful childhood places with each other. These special memories helped nurture the peace, tranquility, and comfort we craved. They were the long-ago days when reality was a familiar friend and not the fearsome stranger it had suddenly become.

And in those moments, as the landscape outside my window became increasingly familiar and I neared my ancestral stomping grounds, the memories I loved the most, the ones of our family's cabin on the river, became more and more vivid.

Lorraine's Lakehouse Memory

Sharon, I think your suggestion of sharing our safe-place memories is a wonderful way of coping with this frightening new world we find ourselves in. I'll tell you of my place, and I hope you'll share yours. Knowing you, it will involve some unusual locale and wild storyline — compared to mine, that is.

My most beloved memories, my go-to peaceful places, are, of course, set in nature. It is where I have always found solace. My childhood safe place was our wonderful but simple family cabin on the Tennessee River.

My parents, with a little help from local tradesmen, built our cabin with their own hands. At the time, it wasn't what I would call rough, but it sure wasn't fancy either. But for me and my siblings, as well as the friends and cousins who came to visit and play in the lake, it was perfect.

We called it the lake, but actually it was the Tennessee River, which, when dammed, formed giant lakes in areas as it flowed through Alabama.

What we children loved most was the dock that stretched fifty feet out into the water. We'd spend hours and hours jumping off that dock, outdoing each other with our cannonballs and clumsy diving attempts.

My parents would sit on the dock, drinks in hand, watching our performances and cheering us on. I remember being horribly obnoxious, calling out over and over, "Mama, watch! . . . Mama, watch!"

That old dock, even at night, provided us kids with entertainment. My father had rigged up a light bulb on the end of a fishing pole, and he would extend it out over the water. The fish loved swimming in circles under the light at night, and we kids loved watching them do it.

The river had all kinds of fish — bass, shad, bream, perch, and, of course, catfish — but at night, under the light, mostly it was the ugly, scary fish with no names that came to the surface. I wasn't their biggest fan; I loved the sweet little perch and bream.

What we children got the biggest kick out of, though, was my father's nightly performance of shooting hideous growths off some of the bigger fish. He was pretty good at it, too.

There were many things I loved doing with my siblings and the other children from neighboring cabins, but the one thing I would not let them in on were my walks on the old dirt road running through the pines behind the cabins.

Those hours spent alone — walking, picking blackberries, listening to the birds, and breathing the clean pine air — were not to be shared. They were mine and mine alone.

One of my more enduring memories of the lake is of a hermit, Old Jake, who lived right on the edge of the dirt road. His ramshackle place was way down where the cabins ended and the quiet, uninhabited, unusable, washed-out road began.

To my young mind, he was mysterious and fascinating, but to the other children, he was just a scary old man. Whenever they saw him, they'd run and torment each other, chanting, "Old Jake is going to get you."

But when I passed his dilapidated, asphalt-shingled shack, I only wished for a glimpse, just a small peek, at his gnarly, bearded, ancient face.

I was never afraid, just more and more intrigued, especially as I grew older. Who was this man, and what had driven him into this existence? What was the catalyst? Now that I'm an adult, I can think of many experiences in life that could drive a person into a life of solitude..

Years later, I thought of visiting Old Jake's shack, but I knew it would be gone, and those who might have known his story are, unfortunately, no longer with us. I'll just have to content myself with my own conclusions and imaginations as to why he chose to live such an undignified, lonely life.

Now and then, making up histories is more enjoyable than the truth. That he was mentally ill is the obvious conclusion, but being me, I prefer romantic tales of heartbreak, societal rejection, and sorry disappointments that drove him to that shack at the end of an obscure Alabama dirt road.

Sharon, I've been writing a screenplay about Old Jake and hope to finish it once Pearl and I are settled in San Miguel. One of the many luxuries I'll have once I give up my business responsibilities. Yahoo!

I experimented with your suggestion of meditation and had an amazing time conjuring up visual memories of the cabin on the lake. After a while, I was in a trancelike state and could literally, in my mind's eye, see everything — its walls, the framed, cheesy 1960s art, the floors, the rugs, the kitchen cabinets; as I opened the cabinets' doors, I saw Ritz crackers, potato chips, Oreos, and all the other favorite junk food we kids adored.

I saw the tacky, simple furniture, the fireplace with the driftwood mantelpiece, but, most of all, the big, indoor, black picnic table we gathered around to eat our eggs, bacon, and biscuits with gravy breakfasts, our baloney sandwich and potato chips lunches, and our catfish and hushpuppy dinners. Life expectancies in the South,

back then at least, were not very long, for obvious reasons — hell, I never ate broccoli until I left home.

All those wonderful images in my subconscious — I can see how this kind of meditation could become addictive. It worked beautifully in quieting my thoughts and soothing my fears.

I am worried for our world, Sharon.

Sharon's Childhood Tennessee Farm

I was right there with you, Lorraine — swimming in the murky lake, exploring the dirt road you walked alone — yes, you and I are cut from the same cloth, except your cloth is probably considered antique-ish by now, unlike mine, which is still very au courant, extremely beautiful, and rare!

Though my story for you today is not outrageous in the least, I feel sure you'll identify with my tomboy days on our seventy-five-acre farm nestled in the hills of Tennessee.

This was a weekend place where my father could play farmer and forget his business woes. For me, it was a chance to play with farm animals and love them like they were my pets.

We had the most fabulous barn on that farm, in which I immediately found a room no one cared about and made it my secret place.

The raw wood smelled wonderful, and it reminded me of the wooden-plank houses on my favorite western shows. But, most of all, it was a place

where I could fantasize and pretend. I loved that barn.

Weather permitting, the family would pile into the car every Saturday morning and drive the forty-five minutes to the farm. I got new cowboy boots, flannel shirts and jeans every fall, just to wear for those outings. I can't remember what my mother or sisters did on those weekends, but I know my father rode his tractor and planted tobacco, while I played with the animals and hiked the farm's steep country hills with my dog Sally.

I have had a lifelong fascination with rocks and archaeology, which must have been inspired by those days, when I was forever digging holes in the creeks' soft, gritty soil, just to see what I couldn't see on the surface. There were plenty of fascinating things to discover just a few inches down. The land, and likely a lot of that part of Tennessee, was chock-full of rock fossils etched with insects and plants. Had I had more knowledge, I'm sure there were many more amazing things than what I uncovered and understood as a child.

We had cattle, pigs, and chickens. There was a tenant farmer who came with the ownership of the property. He and his family were dirt poor, which now I feel sad about, and the farmer's white-trash daughter was always giving my father the fucking eye.

Even though I was barely twelve at the time, I understood what she was doing, and now, knowing what I learned of my father, he likely took her up

on what she was offering. That is not part of my happy place, so I'll end that memory now.

And just like you, Lorraine, I was a loner when it came to my time in nature, whether it was the farm or forest trails near our city home. I took long walks alone. I'd be gone for hours, but my mother never worried; she knew I had my wits about me. The exception to this unspoken trust happened one day while I was by myself at the pigpen.

A mother sow who had had a litter of probably ten little piglets was fenced in in a large pasture down by the creek. I adored her babies so much that one morning I climbed over the fence to play with them.

The mama sow was way on the other side of the pasture, and I remember thinking I had plenty of time if she decided to head my way. I had no clue how dangerous a sow can be, especially when it comes to her babies. I also had no idea how fucking fast a pissed-off pig could run.

Unbeknownst to me, my mother had been keeping an eye on me from the farmhouse on the hill above the pasture. When she saw me climb over the fence, she began her heroic race to save her little girl. Not only did she see what I was doing, she saw the mama sow see what I was doing.

The gigantic pig had turned in my direction and was running like a bat out of hell, while I nonchalantly played with her piglets.

I'll never forget hearing my mother, as she bolted down the hill, screaming for me to get out of the

pasture. When I heard my mother's yells, I turned and looked in the direction of the sow. Sure enough, a ball of fury with hooves was stampeding toward me.

Before I could get myself over the fence, I felt a fist at the neck of my new little flannel shirt, and in the nick of time, it hauled my ass over the chicken-wire fence to safety. I was lectured at the top of my mother's lungs for doing something so stupid.

I recall thinking, wow, my mother must really love me. I wonder if all children, even ones like me with adoring parents, are insecure about their parents' love. I sure was.

I discovered by accident, at the age of thirty-five, how much my mother had loved me as a young girl, but that's another story for another time.

A farm-animal recollection that never fails to make me laugh is one of castrating the baby bulls our heifers had every season. These were not dairy cows but meat cows, which makes me sick to think about; I'm a dedicated vegetarian now.

But at the time, I was just a kid loving the time spent with her father; I did not care one bit what we were doing together.

My dad had this strange metal tool that looked like a big set of pliers; when it was closed, a thick green rubber band was fitted onto its prongs. My father would gently walk up to a baby bull, open the prongs, which stretched out the green rubber band, then put the band over the baby bull's balls and

slowly let the pliers go, leaving the band to gradually cut off the blood supply, and voilà, a week or so later, no more baby bull with balls.

I was always upset when my father did this, but he assured me the little bulls never felt pain. What is amusing, though, is that my older sister and I were allowed to give the calves names, and the little bulls always got our current boyfriends' names. Then, a month or so later, we would assist our dad in castrating them.

I wonder if my parents ever saw the irony in this — cutting off our boyfriends' namesake bulls' balls! I'd bet you money they did. I can just hear my dad, Corky, say to my mom, "Mary, we're off to castrate Sharon's little Ricky. See you later!"

We went to our farm not just on Saturdays but on Sundays as well because Nature was my family's church. And when we arrived back home early Sunday evening, tired, dirty, and hungry, my sisters and I would take baths, wash off the farm dirt, and put on fresh, clean pajamas. The family would then gather around the television with our TV dinners and watch *Bonanza*.

There was so much to love and feel affection for on that farm, Lorraine — my parents, my siblings, Sally, my first dog, who roamed the hills with me, the farm's critters, its creek and its mysterious goodies.

Thoughts or fears of fascists and plagues — today's scary realities were as far from my life as the moon.

Our family's Tennessee farm is my go-to place for solace. Those memories calm my fears when the world seems like such an evil, hostile place in which to live.

As my attention slowly eased back to the present, the view out our windows became more familiar with every mile and every turn. Mentally, I zipped through time, imagining this neck of the woods in my youth — me, a spunky young lady recklessly driving a 1959 Chevrolet, to now — me, an intrepid older woman, carefully driving alone with her dog and mannequin in a twelve-foot rental truck to their future in a foreign land.

It was a daunting and emotional experience.

Such is life.

We are all alone, born alone, die alone, and — in spite of True Romance
magazines — we shall all someday look back on our lives and see that,
in spite of our company, we were alone the whole way. I do not say lonely
— at least, not all the time — but essentially, and finally, alone.
This is what makes your self-respect so important,
and I don't see how you can respect yourself if
you must look in the hearts and minds of
others for your happiness.
~ Hunter S. Thompson

Chapter Eleven

To Grandmother's House We Go!

Over the mountain, and through the town, to Granny's house we go!

My paternal grandmother had an exquisite brick and gingerbread-trimmed Victorian house located in the historic district of my hometown. It was then, and still is, the prettiest part of town, which, unfortunately, is now considered a small city.

While I was growing up in the nineteen sixties in this once small town, it was sometimes referred to as "Rocket City," because of the major local industry of making rockets for NASA. There was and still is one of the first rockets ever made standing tall at the edge of town. As a child, it looked so huge and space-agey to me, but now, sixty years later, I can't help but laugh and see it as just an outdated, big toy.

I had booked a room for Pearl and me at a bed-and-breakfast in one of downtown's historic houses, for four days and three nights. This stay was to be a much-needed break for the two of us weary travelers. It was also a long-planned reunion with my oldest and dearest friends who still lived in town. What's more, a good friend from the island was to fly down, meet us at the B&B, and accompany us for the remainder of the drive to Laredo, Texas.

So much to look forward to, until covid and Hurricane Ida got in the way. Yes, the God Who Laughs was having a good time at the expense of the woman who constantly and optimistically made plans.

Because the road ahead was recognizable from my childhood, I easily found my way over the mountain and to the throughfare that rolled into the old part of town.

I took my time and meandered through the beautiful, tree-lined streets that showcased the most gorgeous historic homes one has ever seen.

Most of these houses, which predate the Civil War, still exist because the Union Army took possession of the town during the war. They confiscated the big, privately owned mansions, and while the Union generals lived in them, the soldiers pitched tents on their immaculate lawns. This is the only reason these homes were not burned to the ground like most of the grand old manors in the South.

I loved that old brick Victorian house of my Granny's. I can see every room in it, and I can still smell the closet where she kept her stinky shoes. Boy, did her feet stink!

It was a real source of embarrassment for her, particularly when she would catch my sister and me pinching our noses and saying "phew" as we held up one of her shoes. She'd then chase us out of the house, shouting, "Bad girls!" while we "bad girls" laughed hysterically on our way out the back door.

As I got older, I began to suspect my Granny was an alcoholic — unfortunately, so was my dad, and, eventually, so was I. But there was something more scandalous: the family began to realize that, in addition to being a boozer, she was also a promiscuous old lady.

She announced one day that, since her house was too large for just one person, she would "rent rooms" to single gentlemen, one old geezer at a time. And after a few months, each tenant became a tenant with fringe benefits.

It was quite hilarious for us — me, my sisters, my parents, aunt, uncle, and cousins — to watch her pretend that these single men were just paying guests and nothing more.

Yes, it was fun and games, until one morning, ole Granny found one of her gentlemen friends dead in bed. That was not funny. I think her room-renting days were over after that upsetting incident. It was sad; everyone liked Mr. Bedford, and we had hopes that he would become more than just one of her "guests." He had become a dotting grandfather figure to all seven of her grandchildren.

I loved my philandering, alcoholic Granny. She was quite the colorful old lady, but referring to her as an old lady is strange, because I am pretty sure I am now several years older than she was at the time.

I parked our truck on the street in front of the bed-and-breakfast and checked us in. To be honest, the house was creepy. Oh well, it was in the part of town I loved, and one of my best friends had recently bought a historic home only a few blocks away. On this first night, which turned out to be our only night, she and another best friend decided we should all mask up and visit each other, Delta covid be dammed.

Earlier in the day, while driving through town looking for the B&B, I had unexpectedly found myself on Granny's street. Upon seeing her wonderful old home, I pulled over, parked in front, and reminisced for a while.

This gorgeous brick house had a classic wraparound, gingerbread-trimmed front porch, the setting for many warm, fun memories, especially the one of me and my older sister and our newly bought Ken doll.

During the very early days of the pandemic, Sharon and I had also shared a few of our childhood doll stories. This particular narrative told the story of my first boy doll, and what my older sister and I did to the poor thing on Granny's porch.

The memory of that hilarious, but charming little scene was as strong and clear as if it had happened yesterday.

Lorraine and Her Big Sister's Destructive Little Hands

Remembering our childhood safe places with each other, Sharon, was really helpful. So I thought, let's share a few doll stories! Hum, maybe you didn't play with them. I know you were a tomboy, but even tomboys are known to have played with dolls.

Well, here goes mine, whether you have a reciprocating story or not. And knowing you, you'll love what my sister and I did to our first Ken doll, one hot summer day on my Granny's old Victorian porch.

I was the biggest Barbie addict in the neighborhood; I adored that doll. She was, hands down, the catalyst for my aspirations and dreams of becoming a fashion designer. Her diminutive outfits — I had them all — were inspired by the great designers, including Dior and Balenciaga.

I played with that doll until I was seventeen and would babysit the little girl across the street for free because she had three Barbies; more importantly, she had loads of her fabulous clothes.

I still have two of the catalogs that featured her amazing wardrobe. In my retail-store days, I would show this tiny brochure to a few select customers. We'd sit on my store couch and become little girls again, pointing to the Barbie outfits we had. What was revealing was how the "career" clothes we children had chosen for Barbie eerily predicted who we became later in life.

Barbie's boyfriend, Ken, came on the scene when I was around ten, and naturally, I had to have him. My sister and I went to Granny's house one Saturday, where she completely surprised us with money to buy a Ken doll. We excitedly walked the few blocks to the Woolworth's store downtown and bought our first boy doll ever.

The minute we got back to the house — I clearly remember — the first thing we did was pull down his miniature pants with the teeny zipper. We were so disappointed in Mattel, the maker of Ken, because we knew what the real deal looked like — on several occasions, we had accidently seen our daddy's fascinating pee-pee.

Feeling ripped off, we attacked the poor, newly bought doll's head. We gleefully picked off all his fuzzy, glued-on hair. And just as we had the innocent guy's head plucked clean, my granny stepped out onto the porch.

To her horror, her two precious granddaughters were holding in their destructive little hands their brand-new, now naked and bald doll. I can still hear her screaming, "What are you girls doing to that thing?"

Needless to say, it was a long time before I got my next Ken doll, and most likely, I had to pay for it myself. I have no memory of what happened to the first doll, but I feel sure Granny made us take it home to our mother and show her what her "bad girls" had done to their new doll.

Sharon, I hope you have a doll tale to tell; our storytelling helps my days feel slightly more normal, whatever normal is.

I can't remember anymore.

Pearl and I walked my hometown's old downtown streets for a while before meeting up with my friends. And I have to say, it was quite nostalgic for me to be in the present day with my beautiful canine companion in the charming old neighborhood stomping grounds I knew as a child.

Time is an enigma. I have sixty-year-old memories that are nearly as strong as a moment ago. It is as if there is only a thin veil between then and now, so much so that sometimes I reach out to an imaginary curtain, pretending to pull it back, hoping for a fleeting glimpse of the past. I wish someday I could step through that imaginary curtain. And given the chance, and depending on the day, I might never come back.

I visited my two best high school friends, but for only a short while. Sadly, as we sat outside, masked up, longing to hug each other, it became just too awkward and surreal. After less than twenty minutes, we reluctantly gave up our charade of normality, and Pearl and I walked back to the B&B.

As the saying goes, you can make new friends, but you cannot make old friends. I wonder, will I make new friends in San Miguel?

That simple but curious question would haunt me many months later in unexpected and heartbreaking ways.

Truly great friends are hard to find, difficult to leave, and impossible to forget.
~ G. Randolf

Chapter Twelve

And God Laughs

When Pearl and I returned from visiting my high school friends, being the news junkie that I am, I put the local news station on and got a big surprise from the God Who Laughs at innocent humans who dare to make plans.

There was an enormous, and I mean enormous, hurricane heading toward Alabama. I had planned to stay in my hometown for a few more days while waiting for my island friend to fly in and help with the remainder of the drive to Laredo.

Making the situation more dire, the hurricane, now named Ida, was barreling not only toward Alabama but also along the exact path we were to take through Mississippi, Louisiana, and Texas.

Shit.

I left a message for my unfortunately soon-to-be-canceled traveling companion, explaining the weather conditions and that we needed an alternate plan for our rendezvous. While waiting for her reply, I recalled Sharon's doll story in response to my Ken doll story.

It was quite an interesting tale she told.

Sharon's Missouri Rag Doll Story

Lorraine, the doll pervert, that was an amusing story of you and your sister assaulting poor Ken, and it just so happens, I do have my own doll story to share with you.

But, first, I want to say, your Granny was a real fucking trip, stinky feet and all. What an interesting character she must have been.

My father's family were longtime Missourians; they went way back in that state's history. My sister and I had never met any of our aunts, uncles, or cousins from that side of the family, so when they threw a family reunion in Missouri, naturally my family went.

I vaguely remember our cousins, but I definitely remember two of our great-aunts. They stitched many things, one being little rag dolls made from scraps with long black yarn for hair.

Before we arrived in St. Louis, they had made one doll for my sister and me to share. I'll repeat that, Lorraine: *one* fucking doll for two young girls.

At the family picnic, these great-aunts presented us with their adorable handmade doll. And later in the day, they taught us how to French braid the rag doll's yarn hair. That was such a mistake, although for me, it became an invaluable life lesson that I have never forgotten.

After the reunion, we piled into our big, old, heavy Buick and began the long trip home. And since superhighways did not exist back then, there was no avoiding driving through every town along the way, which meant stopping at every single traffic light.

My sister and I, riding in the back seat, had been taking turns braiding the hair on this stupid doll, which I had begun to resent.

We fussed and fought over the thing, and I was getting sick of it, but who was really getting sick of it were, of course, my parents.

Our mother, unbeknownst to my sister and me, had secretly made a plan with our father. Since it was summer and cars in the fifties had no air-conditioning, the windows naturally were rolled down.

While we were stopped at one of the town's lights, she turned to my father, gave him a wink, and just when the light turned green, she whipped around, grabbed the little rag doll from my hands, and tossed the annoying thing out the window!

Lorraine, I distinctly remember my father throwing his head back and laughing hysterically as he smashed down on the gas pedal. Obviously, they had plotted and planned this maneuver a few lights back.

My sister burst into tears, but me? I remember being relieved and thinking, good riddance to that silly doll and its dumb braided hair. I also recall admiring my mother for brilliantly solving the problem and making the remainder of the ride home a more peaceful one.

Flash forward forty years — a good friend had given me a private psychic phone session for my birthday. She highly recommended this woman, so I took her up on it. During the session, the psychic said, "Do you remember a particular incident with a doll when you were a young girl?"

At first, I thought, what nonsense; of course, all women have doll stories in their past. Then, suddenly, I recalled the Missouri rag doll story and told the woman my reaction to what my mother had done at the time.

The psychic said, "Sharon, you've been doing the same thing ever since."

She explained what she meant — that, as a young girl, I saw this action as a way to rid oneself of an adverse situation and move on. In other words, toss the negative out, move on and grow from the experience.

After this remarkable session with the psychic, Lorraine, I have referred to this childhood event as "Throwing the doll out the window." And I have done this deed dozens of times throughout my life with men, friends, and anyone who has become more problematic than they are worth. Personally, I think this ability is a positive thing.

Thank you, parents, but most of all, thank you, dear, departed great-aunts, for your unintentional role in this invaluable life lesson.

This, Lorraine, is my one and only doll story, but what a story to remember.

I heard from my now-postponed traveling companion. We agreed that if I waited for her to get to Alabama, the hurricane would be upon us, and it would be days before we could get on the road and make our way southwest to Laredo.

She canceled her ticket and booked a flight a few days later to San Antonio. I then whipped out my trusty Rand McNally and began mapping out a new route that hopefully steered clear of Ida's path.

The God Who Laughs may have thought this was funny, throwing a hurricane monkey wrench into my plans, but I am not only a survivor, I am an old survivor who is still confident and quick on her feet.

Some of us think holding on makes us strong;
but sometimes it is letting go.
~ Herman Hesse

Chapter Thirteen

Outrunning Ida

I knew the right decision was to leave, but to make sure, I called several Alabama friends for advice. After those short conversations with trusted old high school friends, I felt certain that we had to get the hell out of Dodge. The weather report had become more ominous by the hour, and there would be no avoiding the consequences if we continued to stay for even half a day. It was time to hit the road, Jack, and quick.

Our new route's initial start was completely out of the way — a seventy-mile stretch south, in the wrong direction, toward Birmingham. But it was a better alternative than traveling north to Tennessee, then west on dubious back roads all the way to Memphis.

Once Pearl got her business done, I quickly packed up, and the two of us joined Agatha in our cozy home on wheels. We did the route south and, an hour later, linked up to a new interstate going north.

This road was the most glorious highway I saw during my entire trip through a good portion of the States and halfway down the length of Mexico.

I had begun to rate the condition of each state's roads, and Alabama won hands down. Understandably, the roads up north were worse, by far; I chalked this up to the more severe winter weather. There was one word I found myself saying over and over — *infrastructure!*

Besides this one stretch of road in Alabama, potholes were everywhere, but even more dangerous were the ripped and shredded tires, spun off from large trucks, lining the sides of the interstate. It was truly unbelievable. The piles and piles of black rubber strewn about were something I had never seen before. Why they had not been cleaned up puzzled me. Covid?

I began to worry about being behind an eighteen-wheeler when one of their giant tires blew — what happens to a car or truck behind them when they shred off? I saw what happens firsthand in Texas the following day. Luckily, the tire remnants went under the small car without causing any harm, and the driver was able to pull off the road. It was a frightening thing to watch.

As I was heading toward Birmingham, a story exchange between Sharon and me came to mind. Once again, bored with thinking about the long road ahead, I began indulging in recollections of our early teenage years while growing up in the South.

Though we had both been raised below the Mason-Dixon Line, neither of us had really seen much of the hateful, racist events that occurred during the nineteen fifties, sixties, and early seventies.

While Sharon was much younger than me, she still had been brought up in the Deep South, which, even today, is infected with plenty of racial animosity.

The day did come, though, when we both encountered bigotry up close and personal. It could have been worse; nevertheless, it was not pretty.

Lorraine's Birmingham Bus Station Story

I am so glad, Sharon, that we both grew up in the South; there is a commonality we share that is near impossible to have with — okay, I'll say it: a Yankee!

And, like you, I experienced very little racism in my youth. Although I am certain I knew what it looked and sounded like, I can't say that I knew what it felt like, having been a little white girl of privilege.

I sure got a taste of it, though, when I moved up North and lived among Northern people. Back then, to them, anyone with a Southern accent was considered stupid and less-than. How I resented those ignorant people with their misguided assumptions.

Growing up in Alabama, my hero was Martin Luther King Jr. In fact, the great man figures in one of my favorite childhood memories. You know, the kind of memory where you stop and think, damn, I was a good kid.

It happened while I was in a bus station, getting ready to board a Greyhound traveling from northern Alabama to New Orleans. I must have been all of fifteen and was on my way to help my Aunt Betty, whose cheating husband had left her and their four children for another woman. Men. I could give you my "Why I love menopause" sermon right now, but I'll save it for later.

My Aunt Betty, who I'm pretty sure had never worked a day in her life, was suddenly thrown into the world of work and needed a week's training for the only place that would hire her. So, on my very own, I volunteered to babysit my cousins for a week.

I distinctly remember having the idea and proudly announcing to my mom one morning, "I want to go to New Orleans and help Aunt Betty." I also recall thinking, "What are you doing? It's your summer vacation."

But the words were already out of my mouth, and my mother, in shock, was thrilled that her selfish little girl had come up with this selfless, generous plan all on her own. How could I disappoint my mom? I loved her to pieces, so I had to follow through with my spur-of-the-moment generosity.

Several weeks later, it is 1966, I'm fifteen, alone, and sitting in a Birmingham, Alabama, bus station. Besides summer camp, I think this was my first time on my own — I mean really, by-myself-away-from-home alone. I remember: something got into me, something feisty, mischievous, and slightly reckless. Maybe it was because I was miles from home, but I had a need to act out. It's strange when you remember a feeling; it's different from a visual memory.

I had spotted a paperback book rack in front of a newspaper stand inside the station. Positioned in the front of the rack, and in a clear shot to my line of sight, was a book with Martin Luther King Jr.'s face on it. I can't remember the title. It didn't matter to me; it was his face I was interested in.

I bought the book, then sat down on a wooden bench for all the other passengers in the waiting room to see me, a little white girl reading a book about a controversial black man. I held the book proudly in front of my face, pretending I was reading, and every so often, I'd do the classic peek over the top of the book to see if anyone was watching.

I was hoping to offend anyone who could possibly be offended, and if my memory is correct, I was being quite obnoxious about it and received plenty of hateful stares. Who was this sassy young Caucasian girl who would be so provocative as to read such a thing in a public place in the heart of the South in 1966?

That girl was me, and I laugh to myself every time I see that scene in my mind's eye.

Sharon's Bigoted White-Trash Waitress Confrontation

Lorraine, I loved your story of the young white girl provoking Southern racists in the bus station. And, of course, I've been racking my brain for my own story of equal defiance. I did remember one I'll tell you about; it's similar, but I don't think as courageous as yours.

Like you, I grew up in a small town in the South, with liberal, outspoken parents. I was a dancer with the Civic Ballet Company before I bravely struck off for the Big Apple at eighteen.

I too was alone when I went, but I was quite a bit older than you when you took your out-of-character, good-deed bus trip to New Orleans. In all honesty, though, New York City is a hell of a lot scarier than a Birmingham bus station, no matter how old you are.

So here's my modest story of chutzpa: I can't remember my age; maybe I was sixteen. Anyway, the ballet company I belonged to rehearsed all day on Saturdays, and while my high school chums shopped at the mall or did whatever the fuck they did, I danced my ambitious butt off.

I had ballet classes during the week, but on Saturdays, I was forever learning some new ballet and preparing for my future in dance. And even though I was not the best ballet dancer, by far, my dedication and determination went a long way; more important, it got me the hell out of the town I grew up in.

I have never been one to let obstacles get in my way — say, like not being naturally talented — but when I know, without a doubt, that this is my path, this is my future, look out. Impediments are for the fearful, don't you think?

One Saturday, the one black dancer in our ballet company and I went to the shitty greasy-spoon restaurant next door. It abutted the parking lot of the dilapidated old school building that housed the Arts Council, where we danced.

Lorraine, it must have been the first time the two of us had gone together to this dive, because we never would have returned for a second helping of this racist bitch's shit.

We sat down at the counter to order, and the red-neck, trashy white waitress refused to serve my black friend. You may think this was common in the South, and it was, but it was the first time I had experienced this behavior in a person.

This was the early 1970s, for Christ's sake. I said, "Well, then, you cannot fucking serve me either, you fucking, white-trash-cracker-bitch," and we got up and left.

Except for my poor mother, I think that was the first time I ever said the word "fuck" to anyone's face. I do remember rehearsing my cussing as I drove around at breakneck speeds in my old, beat-up, red Chevy Impala.

Of course, I had the windows rolled up, as if that made me less crazy. Yep, I would ride around

practicing my full-throated art of profanity in that sleezy, hand-me-down car. What a sight I must have been!

Boy, I'd kill for that car today; as tacky as it still seems to me, it's a true American classic. And, believe this or not, my monkey, Ralph — yes, I had a monkey — would sit on my shoulder and ride around with me. I kid you not.

Remind me to tell you more about Ralph the monkey as well as Ralph, my monkey's namesake, who took my virginity at eighteen in his old Ford station wagon. The adorable sexpot drove around with a mattress in the back of his infamous bedroom on wheels. What an asshole, and I fell for it.

Back to the diner: my black friend and I got the hell out of there. We returned to the ballet rehearsals and told all the other dancers about the cracker waitress and her racist ways. And, let me tell you, none of us dancers ever ate at that fucking place again. Well, at least no one admitted to it.

Okay, that story isn't as defiant as yours, but, hey, it was the beginning of my career in openly swearing and seriously dancing.

Lorraine, I'm beginning to believe I'll never outgrow my sailor's mouth. Do you think maybe, possibly, I have a mild case of Tourette's syndrome? My mother used to say I did.

I'm really kind of serious about this; these terrible words just slip right out, and I feel oh so good as

they do. There are worse personality defects, I guess. Maybe I need to stop watching so much Netflix.

The gratuitous cursing is really over the top on a lot of their shows; even I am offended sometimes. I've noticed my use of depraved language is escalating, which, incidentally, coincides with my recent Netflix binging.

I've heard that, as you age, your ability to retrieve words diminishes. I figure that, eventually, I will either have trouble remembering the curse words and speak like normal people (except those on Netflix) or be left with only bad language.

I think it would be tragic for a person like me to have a vocabulary of only good, normal words, don't you?

The enjoyable part of long-distance driving, for me, was the luxury of fantasizing; it was an indulgence that was unfamiliar to me.

I had been an extremely hardworking woman and was fortunate that my work was creative, but, nevertheless, it consumed all my waking hours. And unless I was in the woods with my dogs, to allow my mind to be in the clouds for any length of time was a guilty pleasure I had rarely known.

I think the second-best part of the trip, though, was the simple act of driving. It was essentially the only thing I had to do. There were no phone calls to make, no mother-of-the-bride dresses to worry about, no mortgage to fret over, it was a clear-cut linear task — get myself and Pearl from point A to point B.

Even long before I left the island, I was looking forward to the (hopefully) uncomplicated driving days ahead of me.

I was keeping tabs on Hurricane Ida from the stations I managed to find on the truck's not-so-great radio. I was relieved that I had left when I did; Ida was absolutely headed our way, but my new route, in all likelihood, was out of her path. The Saint Christopher medal, blessed by a priest, was doing its job, and I was grateful for it.

Though my tired, old, road-weary butt was still giving me trouble now and then, the pain was subsiding and becoming more tolerable each day.

Thirty more miles to Memphis, then due west to Little Rock — two cities that would become slightly problematic, and not the least bit fun.

All I've ever wanted, since I was a child,
was to do something wonderful.

~ Patti Smith

Chapter Fourteen

Memphis Surprise!

After more than a thousand miles of driving, I finally felt relaxed and less on edge. I had been tense since my first stop in Harrisburg, Pennsylvania, where I picked up I-81. My nervousness was understandable; the constant barrage of trucks around me had been relentless. But now, traveling on this stretch of Alabama highway, I felt at ease and was able to enjoy the beautiful, landscaped views.

For fifty miles, I had had this beautiful road, if a road can be such a thing, almost completely to myself. Then suddenly, surprise! A sign appeared out of nowhere saying, *Road ends in two miles.* A small but significant detail Rand McNally was apparently not up to date on.

Damn. Now what?

Seeing no option but to keep driving north, I said a little prayer to Saint Christopher and kept the pedal to the metal. When the two miles came to an abrupt end, five miles outside of Memphis, ten or so big trucks were piled up ahead of us. The obvious thing to do was to follow the truckers, who I felt sure knew their way through the city, and that's what I did.

The outskirts of Memphis are a real crap-hole, but then again, most outlying areas of medium-size to large cities in the United

States are crap-holes. And, lucky me, the trucker I happened to be behind seemed to know his way to the East–West interstate hidden deep inside the bowels (pun intended) of Memphis.

If my memory is correct, the one and only time I had ever been in Memphis was with my Granny, the alcoholic, promiscuous grandmother with stinky feet. She had taken my sister and me there to enjoy one of the riverboat rides on the Mississippi River, but most of all, we were there to visit Graceland, the home of Elvis.

This was our first trip alone with Granny, and we were so excited. Elvis, my first crush's home, yippee! Little did we seven- and eight-year-old girls know, our Granny was also a maniacal control freak.

She had long, sharp, red fingernails, and whenever we did something, anything really, that annoyed her, she would pinch our earlobes until they bled. It was very painful, and by the time we got back home to our mother, there were scabs all over our poor, pitiful ears.

However, that alone wasn't what truly enraged our mother. Her mother-in-law had cut off our beautiful, shoulder-length curls and given us pixie haircuts! I think they were popular back then, but my sister and I knew what she was really up to. She cut off our gorgeous hair to get better access to our now pinched-to-pieces little ears!

My mother never allowed us to travel alone with Granny again. I also remember my mother banning her from coming to our cabin on the lake.

She was terrified of water, and whenever we dove under the surface, she would scream at the top of her lungs, "Help, the children are drowning! Help, the children are drowning! Come quick!"

Mother was determined for her children to have as few fears as possible, one being the fear of water. So fearful, stinky-footed, ear-pincher Granny was never allowed to visit our cabin on the lake again.

Pearl and I made it through Memphis in one piece. I say this because it was not an easy route to negotiate, especially when the truck we were following suddenly disappeared. Once out of this nerve-racking, truck-infested city, we headed toward Little Rock, our next overnight hotel stay.

Fortunately, we got to the hotel before dark, but unfortunately, there was another surprise in store for us. This place, part of the same wonderful chain of pet-friendly hotels we had been staying in, was disgusting — a horrible, gross, smelly dive. However, Pearl and I were tired and hungry, and it was only for a night.

But phew-wee!

Adversity is sometimes hard upon a man;
but for one man who can stand prosperity,
there are a hundred that will stand adversity.
~ Elvis Presley

Chapter Fifteen

Sleepless in Little Rock

Maybe there was a full moon that night . . . maybe I had eaten too many chocolate-covered expresso beans that day . . . conceivably, it was the high-anxiety drive to escape Hurricane Ida . . . or it could have been the nail-biting interstate run through Memphis.

But, possibly, and more likely, it was the unbelievable, horrible smell of our grungy hotel room. Whatever the reason, I could not, for the first time on our trip, fall asleep.

And so, not being able to sleep, I lay back, got comfortable, and read transcripts from two of my favorite Sharon and Lorraine exchanges.

My story was about what I saw as a wonderful pandemic bonus, and Sharon's story was another one of her going-to-the-slammer tales.

I thought I might regret doing this, but the long, albeit lively narratives brought back such memorable times that, before I knew it, I was dreaming happy dreams of colorful feathered creatures being merrily chased by long-haired cops dressed in faded jeans.

Lorraine's Pandemic Wild Turkey Perk!

Sharon, in all honesty, because of the quick onslaught of this pandemic, I cannot shake the impression that the world we once knew is fading before our eyes, and there is nothing we can do to stop it. Will our pre-pandemic reality be gone forever, and if so, what will the post-pandemic reality look like? Will the world have changed so much we won't even recognize it?

Doom and gloom, I'm sorry to say, is my constant companion these days. And this slow-motion disaster is real, not a narrative on a screen where we can flip the dial, watch something else, or simply turn it off and walk away.

Sharon, for decades, I've worried about threats from Mother Nature because of the brutality humans daily force on her, and some mornings, nature and my dogs are the only reason for getting out of bed.

Every living thing in this world is elegantly linked to every other living thing — the chaos theory of the butterfly effect. You know, when a butterfly flaps his wings in India, a hurricane is created in the West Indies. Of course, that's an exaggeration, but you get the concept.

I like what Benjamin Franklin wrote in "The Way to Wealth":

> For want of a nail the shoe was lost,
> For want of a shoe the horse was lost,
> For want of a horse the rider was lost,
> For want of a rider the battle was lost,
> For want of a battle the kingdom was lost,
> And all for the want of a horseshoe nail.

Somewhere, someone, innocently, I hope, messed up with this virus, and now the world is paying dearly for it — the chaos butterfly effect.

One out of the many bizarre new things brought on by the pandemic is the fear people have of being a few feet from each other, and for someone like me, who naturally touches the person I am talking to, and who hugs for no reason, it is uncomfortable and confusing. Most of my adult life, I have been a person who does not shy away from people, so my self-esteem, everyone's self-esteem, is suffering from this terrible new unnatural social norm.

But as with every adversity in life, there can be a silver lining if you are open to it. My favorite among the pandemic's perks (as I call them), which has thrilled us all, are the wildlife that live near urban areas and how they have come out to play now that the normally dominating humans are hiding in their houses.

In my little town, Sharon, the wild turkeys, which I have always adored, have taken to the streets, and it has been hilarious for me and my neighbor.

March and April are the months in the Northeast when the male turkeys begin to preen and show off their gorgeous tail feathers. Whomp! is the sound their tail feathers make when they fully spread. The joy of that sight and sound will never become old for me.

There is one old male turkey I call Gus who proudly preens for anyone he can corner. Half of his tail feathers are chewed up or missing from a lifetime of turkey combat, yet he sashays and swaggers like he is the most handsome turkey in town! I love old Gus.

These amazing ground birds, which can actually fly high into the trees when they are frightened or when they roost for the night, usually kept to people's backyards and the town cemetery. But because of the lockdown, cars on the streets are few and people out and about even fewer. Subsequently, the turkeys have made our streets their stage to preen and show off their gorgeous feathered goods.

I looked out the window the other morning, and there were no less than nine male turkeys whomping and flashing their tail feathers while strutting in the middle of the once-busy road in front of my house.

I called my neighbor, who also loves these comical creatures, to stop what she was doing and look out her window. We were entertained for hours.

This magnificent little turkey parade, on the road in front of our homes, was a pandemic silver lining, for sure.

Sharon's May Day
Going to the Pokey Story

Yes, Lorraine, it seems our world has turned the fuck upside down. And yet you are right, there are amusing and wonderful things happening everywhere simultaneously with the scary stuff we hear day in and day out.

And not only, as you point out, are they entertaining, unusual goings-on; they also are sanity-saving miracles occurring in full view of our fearful, tired eyes.

It's as if, suddenly, an unexpected, dangerous storm blew in and has no intention of leaving. You adjust to its threats, its unpredictability, but it's always there, wherever you go. There is just no fucking getting away from it. How can we not all be frightened?

For a distraction, how about I tell you another one of my incarceration stories? This one took place in D.C., and maybe it will cheer you up, take your mind off the world's possible, soon-to-be Armageddon. Or is it a soon-to-be Apocalypse? I get the movies mixed up. Hey, whoever is running this shit show: which fucking movie are we in? We'd all like to know.

So, I was in New York, it was months before my move to California, and, in my own sort of way, I was still working on my dance career.

I was living with my best friend, Sheila, and her boyfriend, Paul, on Third Street in the East Village, the dream address of every serious Manhattan hippie.

Paul was a very successful and extremely active marijuana dealer at the time. And he had the largest afro I had ever seen on a white person, especially a Jewish white person.

I felt so cool, and as a certified cracker from the South, I was certain I had reached the pinnacle of hippie success by attending concerts at the Filmore East whenever they had a show; I didn't care who was playing, I was there.

Most important, though, I was enthusiastically and regularly spreading my newfound hallucinogenic wings every weekend. But truthfully, in reality, I was throwing away my future in dance.

My career ambitions were sliding, and I was daily lying to myself, saying that once I got to L.A., things would be different, and I would buckle down and make up for my slacking off.

Before moving in with Paul and Sheila, I had gone back home and bought my infamous used white Econoline van. I was parking it on the street near our basement Village apartment. In the mornings, no matter how well I had locked the thing up the night before, bottles and food wrappers were strewn inside it — crap obviously left by poor street bums.

They weren't fucking up the vehicle or trying to steal it, so I said, Screw it; who cares? They only want a place to sleep, and little did I know that the back of that van would one day be where I'd lay my own tired head at night.

Paul, who had his finger on the pulse of every important long-hair event on the East Coast, announced one day in May of 1971 that a huge Vietnam War protest in Washington, D.C., called May Day, was taking place starting the coming weekend and extending into the following week.

He then declared that a gang of us were going to drive down there in my van and camp out in Potomac Park. The major radical hippie leaders at the time had not only secured protest permits but also camping permits. How they did that, especially the camping permits, was always a mystery to me.

I was thrilled and honored that my van was to be the vehicle to cart our denim-covered, stoned asses down to D.C. I felt like the neatest, most radical anti-war kid on the block. This was right up my alley, and unbeknownst to me, I had a raging activist inside of me — I mean, raging — and she was about to be set free.

The beginning of May, the Third Street gang piles into my Econoline van, and we head down I-95 to Washington, D.C. I remember very little about the drive, but I'm sure we were all pumped up with heated Nixon bashing and passion-fueled anti–Vietnam War rhetoric.

We found our way to Potomac Park and set up camp. Again, looking back, how the fuck did Tom Hayden and his crew ever get permits from the city of Washington, D.C., for thousands of hippies to swarm its pristine Potomac Park, pitch tents, drive vans onto the grass, and make campfires?

Clearly, this did not last very long. Before we were barely settled in, out of nowhere, helicopters with searchlights were flying overhead, blasting the message for us to get the fuck out. I bet some D.C. park manager who had approved this fiasco had his ass handed to him that night. I'd love to know the backstory on this; maybe it's in someone's memoir by now.

Imagine, tens of thousands of hippies frantically scrambling to leave the park in the pitch black of night. It was chaos — fun, exciting chaos. I have no memory of where we went, but we had a van to sleep in, so that's probably what we did.

The next day, and for the duration of the protest, we lucked out and were invited to stay in gorgeous houses all over town. Dozens of D.C. and Georgetown residents were opening up their homes to the ragtag bands of peace marchers milling around and regrouping on their residential streets.

We May Day war protesters were from all over the country, and the majority of American citizens by now were against the war, no matter their status in life.

So it was no surprise when these non-radical homeowners gave us grungy, ragamuffin, anti-war warriors a place to crash on their elegant Georgetown parquet floors.

Somehow, and without cell phones, we formed large individual groups to block all the entrances into the heart of the city where the government buildings were located.

The people with whom I formed an alliance were the DuPont Circle group. We were tasked with stopping traffic through the circle and into downtown D.C.

I don't know whose idea it was to put nails under city bus tires, because I surely was not the one carrying around four-inch nails in my pocket. But when one of our leaders asked if a few of us would volunteer to do the deed, I, of course, eagerly stepped up to the plate.

I did the deed, and as I was backing up and getting ready to run from the scene of the crime, a huge cop grabbed me around the waist. I kicked and screamed, but I was no match for this giant man and was swiftly thrown into the back of a paddy wagon full of fellow captured comrades.

What a great, wonderful day it was for me and over two hundred thousand anti-war protestors, many of whom proudly went to jail for what they believed in.

I must have been in lockup for at least twenty-four hours when our heroine from New York, Congresswoman Bella Abzug, rode in, wearing one of her famous hats, and made a big, huge fucking stink about our disgusting jail conditions.

We had little food and were crammed into ten- by twelve-foot cells with up to thirty people in each cell. As thrilling as it was, at first, to be locked up together, the excitement quickly turned to misery.

Maybe that was the point, but if so, it proved futile in the end. Because once we were let back out on the streets, we went right at it again and were all thrown in jail for a second time.

With this second jail go-round, the D.C. police were rounding up anyone, and I mean anyone, off the streets and throwing them in the slammer. Now there were not just us radical hippies in jail; there were teenagers who were innocently walking to school and businesspeople walking to work. It was fantastic!

What baffles me, when I look back, is how, in the end, our gang from Manhattan found each other in all the commotion and made our way back to New York. I also haven't a clue as to where the van was for the days we were locked up.

Though this adventure was unnerving at times — I would not trade it for the world.

After a surprisingly decent night's sleep in the smelly motel room, Pearl and I were eager to get back on the road and begin our long drive through Texas. There were to be several more nights' stays at the same chain of hotels as we worked our way to Laredo; thankfully, the rest were top-notch, without any hint of weird odors.

Pearl did her business, and Agatha, of course, looked fresh as a daisy and ready to roll. I happily got myself settled in the truck for another day's drive, which would bring us a day closer to our final destination.

Still, what lay head — crossing the border, driving halfway through Mexico, and closing on our new house — seemed a world away.

You measure a democracy by the freedom it gives its dissidents, not the freedom it gives its assimilated conformists.
~ Abbie Hoffman

Chapter Sixteen

Dallas, Deluges,
and
Despicable Dudes

It was Sunday morning, the fifth day of our trip, and since most of the day would be spent driving through Texas, I called a Vineyard friend who had just driven across the ginormous state.

She immediately warned me of the precarious driving conditions as you approach and negotiate your way through Dallas. She also urged me to look at my map and search for back roads around the city's monstruous tangle of highway construction that, without warning, left you in the middle of nowhere.

This potential but possibly avoidable ordeal reminded me of driving through Memphis. And even though that experience was still fresh in my mind, I felt the need to consult my two passengers as to what to do.

After getting blank stares and zero help, I decided, hell, the worst that could happen was losing time if we got lost. I also reminded myself that I had found my way through the maze of confusion in Memphis on a Saturday, so how hard could it be driving through Dallas on a Sunday?

Fortunately, I was right, but it took all the concentration I could muster. Pearl napped through the worst of it, so I had no distractions from her. I just kept my brain alert, my eyes glued to the road, and my reflexes ready for anything and everything that, without warning, could come our way.

Having gotten through Dallas with flying colors, I figured the worst driving for the day was over, but, oh no, Mother Nature had a big, frightening surprise in store for us.

I had gotten my first real cell phone several months prior to leaving my former life. For years, my friends had chided me for not having one of these soul-stealing gadgets, but I remained adamant in my belief that not only did I not want one, I did not need one.

I was convinced — and as it turned out, I was correct — that I would become one of those pitiful people I had made fun of for decades: addicts who can't be without their stupid phone for five minutes.

Yes, I too had become another one of Pavlov's iPhone dogs. But I was moving to a foreign country, and this dreaded gadget was to become a lifeline to both my past and my future lives, and, of course, it was an absolute necessity for the long, overland journey to Mexico.

Soon after our intense and laser-focused drive through the sprawling city of Dallas, the weather drastically changed. So far, I had not encountered any inclement weather on our trip, which was partly due to luck, but also to my skill in circumventing Hurricane Ida. However, a few miles out of that city's suburbs, my luck changed, and all hell broke loose.

I had had my attention so fixed on navigating the confusing roads ahead that whatever was going on in the sky above had not been on my radar. The air pressure dropped; black, menacing clouds appeared out of nowhere, and the heavens abruptly and violently opened up. Fortunately, like most of the other drivers, I was able to ease the truck safely off the highway. But some vehicles just kept on going, which I found reckless and dangerously foolish.

The rain pelted the truck's roof so hard that I began to imagine the entire top caving in and the deluge ruining my now few worldly possessions. Scared out of my wits, I used my former nemesis, the cell phone, to call the same friend who had warned me about Dallas.

Even though we could barely hear each other over the pounding rain, she kept me company until the storm eased. Since she knew Texas better than I did, I asked her if this sudden torrential rain was a known weather phenomenon in the state.

It wasn't, to her knowledge, so I chalked it up to climate change and hoped it was just a freak, one-time occurrence. It was not. These abrupt, dangerous downpours happened on and off for the next hundred miles or so.

Luckily, I was able to safely get off the road every time the sky opened and put the fear of God into me. This was a different God from the one who laughs; this was the God who gets kicks out of terrifying little humans with nature's frightening powers.

And, honestly, there were moments when I was truly afraid.

During one of these intervals, I was forced to park on an auxiliary road for over an hour. For something to do besides pestering friends on the phone, I cranked the radio volume up high and found myself laughing hysterically to the country-western station I had found back in Arkansas.

I was laughing over the time when Sharon and I had admitted to our secret love of country songs. Since we had both been born and raised in the South, it was natural for us to appreciate this type of music.

Except I had spent my entire adulthood surrounded by Yankees, and it had been a secret that I, understandably, had kept quiet about for many years.

When I first left Alabama, country music was different than today; it was considered a tacky genre only hillbillies and rednecks found entertaining. My appreciation of this great music genre would have been just more cracker-fodder for the Yankee snobs in my life.

While waiting for the rain to ease up, and being in Texas, I thought about the different country songs I loved; a particular one, whose lyrics I knew by heart, kept coming to mind.

It always reminded me of the circumstances that precipitated the end of my drinking days, which again, since we were in Texas, land of cowboys and cowboy hats, prompted another memory — the recollection of the devastating but soul-saving relationship with a man that led to my sobriety.

The song's lyrics that jogged this life-altering memory depicted a cowardly, despicable man who wore a fabulous cowboy hat in the hopes that the manly hat would disguise his gutlessness from the ladies. The tune's tale always reminded me of the saying, "All hat, no cattle." This song was more like, "All hat, no courage."

A year after I had cut ties with the man instrumental in my becoming sober, I heard a great country-western tune on the radio. This song's story was so similar to my sobering-up love affair that I was convinced someone in A.A. had heard my miserable yarn and put it to music.

I realized later that it was just another wonderful woo-woo gift from the Universe. This gift, though, was timed with my first-year sobriety anniversary, and I felt then, and always will, that it was meant to assure me I was on the right path.

This man, my bottom in life — the biggest insult anyone could say to another person — was, to be honest, butt ugly. And so, to help distract from his ugliness, I pleaded with him for months to buy a sexy black cowboy hat I had seen online.

The reason I desperately wanted him to wear this hat was because I thought country-western singers, no matter their looks, were handsome and rugged when they wore cowboy hats.

Call me crazy, I don't care, but I almost had him convinced of how hot and fabulous he'd look, when on television one night there was a clip about Waylon Jennings, whom I adored. I said to my ugly boyfriend, "See how handsome Waylon looks in *his* hat?"

My boyfriend may have been unattractive, but he wasn't stupid. And because of that remark, he realized this little charade of mine was so I could pretend he was Waylon Jennings in bed, and he was right.

Without my knowing it — and, really, how could I have known — this unsightly, despicable, lying, cheating bastard was to be the catalyst for my impending sobriety.

Even more surprising, this piece of shit also had the dubious honor of being the leading man in my "moment of clarity" story.

But all's well that ends well — I was stone-cold sober within ten months of meeting him.

On my sixteenth anniversary, I had shared my hitting bottom saga with Sharon and was glad to, because, once again, it was a story of human adversity with a sparkling, beautiful, silver lining.

I may be crazy, but it keeps me from going insane.
~ Waylon Jennings

Lorraine's Moment of Clarity

Sharon, you've asked several times how I became sober. Well, here is my "moment of clarity" story. That term is what a recovering alcoholic or addict calls the instant it became unquestionably clear that they had to stop living a lie and sober up or die. And the who or what that brought them to their knees and delivered this miracle is the most significant part of any sober alcoholic's story.

My moment of clarity was the day I realized that if I married the man I was engaged to, I was out of my alcohol-marinated mind, and the life that I had worked so hard to keep from ruin would quickly go down the proverbial drain. And for what? A man not even worth shedding a tear over, much less throwing away a life that, at times, I had figuratively bled for.

I was closing in on fifty and suddenly felt alone. This surprised me because loneliness had never been a concern of mine; I enjoyed being solitary. I had plenty of close friends scattered around the country, yet suddenly I had a desperate need for a serious relationship, hopefully with someone who had an extended family. Me craving a family?

I had always run in the opposite direction; men with children and large families were never on my wish list. This new need felt really strange. My single girlfriends and I all had enjoyed our freedom from family responsibilities; it was a premeditated lifestyle we had created for ourselves.

Since my big milestone birthday was looming, I was sure my age was the reason this new, vacuous hole of discontent had opened up. I had begun to feel certain that, with the love of a man, I'd be fulfilled and on my way to a happier, healthier life. I never, ever considered for a minute that this depressing black hole I had been steadily digging was becoming deeper and deeper through my constant, daily drinking.

My friends knew of my troubles, and, interestingly enough, none of them, except my drinking buddy and fiancé, had substance-abuse problems. Normally, this is not the case. Usually, substance abusers surround themselves with equal or, more commonly, worse abusers than themselves.

Well, truthfully, maybe I did too, because the majority of the men in my life had had problems with drugs and alcohol. The reason I chose these men is clear — less judgmental criticism and finger-pointing conversations about my drinking habits. I could look at many things in relation to myself, but not my drinking — anything but that.

Sharon, did you ever experiment with online dating? I did, for years; remind me to tell you about a true horror story with one of the men I met — it will give you goose bumps.

Whenever I joined one of these dating services, inevitably, within weeks of contacting and being contacted, I'd throw in the towel and promise to never to join again. But time would pass, and I'd be full of hope with the possibility that it would be different this time, and try again.

A few days into my sworn last attempt at this, a man whom I had never met on the Vineyard contacted me. This was strange because most of us long-term year-rounders were acquainted with one another. I asked friends if they knew of this man. Most did, and there were mixed reviews, but I decided I had nothing to lose, so I agreed to meet him.

He was a successful artist, a homeowner, a bit older than me; on paper, it seemed like a good match. I had come to the conclusion, after a previous painful relationship with a good-looking man from Texas, that if a man was unattractive, I would be more appreciated and not as emotionally abused.

Ha!

The artist and I emailed, talked on the phone a couple of times, and agreed to meet. I don't think I even knew what he looked like; I was just hoping he was not attractive.

Back then, many people didn't post their photos on the dating sites; that technology wasn't readily available yet. Nevertheless, I met this match-on-paper, and, sure enough, I hit the jackpot; he was unattractive! Actually, to be honest, ugly *would have been the correct adjective.*

It didn't take long, though, before I realized that he was so hard for me to look at, I needed to be totally drunk to sleep with him. I had also discovered that, if I pretended he was a country-western singer and kept my eyes shut, I could get sufficiently turned on.

Eventually, I persuaded him into letting his hair grow, and with very little effort and at his expense, I upgraded his wardrobe. He was definitely a fixer-upper.

Within a few weeks of meeting, we were together every night. And every night I would guzzle a big bottle of wine, something I had been doing on my own for a while, and he'd down glasses of vodka.

I soon came to realize that what was worse than his vodka drinking was his constant pot smoking. And because of our mutual tolerance of each other's substance abuse, we seriously thought we were in love. In reality, though, we were mixing up love with gratitude for the acceptance of each other's addictions.

This shared love/addiction thing went on for months, but even drunk, hungover, and deluded as I was, I knew in my heart that he was a cheater and a pathological liar. I finally caught him red-handed by hacking into his email; I mean, for Christ's sake, who uses their dog's name for their password?

Throughout the long ten months of this relationship misery, there is one visual moment I will never forget. I was absolutely certain he was cheating (this incident was before my email hacking), and I wanted actual evidence to throw in his face.

I needed time alone in his house, and one day, when he drove to town on an errand, I went through his garbage. It was such a humiliating, undignified thing for me to do that I had an out-of-body experience while carrying out the pathetic act.

I could see the entire scene from above — me bending over this horrible man's trash can and anxiously going through it. This fall from grace absolutely freaked me out.

I frantically gathered my dogs and got the hell out of there. During the whole drive back to my house, I said over and over, "You have to end this nightmare. You have to end this nightmare. What is wrong with you?"

It wasn't too long after this trash-can-surfing incident that I went to a therapist recommended by a friend who was a longtime member of Alcoholics Anonymous. Later on, I came to believe, without a doubt, that my friend being in A.A. was no mere coincidence.

I had been seeing this therapist for a month when I finally faced myself and my alcoholism. The woman said to me, "Two things, Lorraine — get as far away from this man as possible, and call your friend who recommended me and go to an A.A. meeting with her. You, my dear, are an alcoholic."

I do give myself credit, though. When I realized the script I had been writing for decades no longer worked, I immediately tore it up and began a new one — one word, one page at a time.

I never looked back; however, I did see him once again, which lasted all of two days. I was sober and could not, with a clear head, conjure up that country-western singer thing any longer. Even a hat, a great big, fabulous black cowboy hat, would not have done the trick.

A switch had been flipped, and I liked it. In fact, I loved it. I was free; I was finally free from alcohol.

Sharon, this is my truthful, unabashed account of becoming sober, and I hope you don't think any less of me, but if you do, it doesn't matter, because frankly, my dear, you're worse than I am!

I have this disease late at night sometimes, involving alcohol and the telephone.
~ Kurt Vonnegut

Though it would be another five hours of driving, I was determind to get to San Antonio before dark. The torrential rains had put my driving time behind by a few hours, but by being off the road and letting my thoughts wander for a while, I actually felt rejuvenated.

If I was able get to San Antonio by nightfall, I could relax and hang out at the hotel; the following day, my neighbor from the island was to arrive, and I had lots to do to get ready for her. She was the same friend who was to meet me in Alabama before Hurricaine Ida chased Pearl, Agatha, and me out of town.

Our alternate plan: meet in San Antonio, stay overnight, drive to Laredo the next day, unload at the movers' storage facility, drop the truck off, stay overnight again, say our goodbyes, then go our separate ways — she back to the Vineyard, Pearl and I over the border, then five hundred miles to San Miguel, our final destination.

That day of goodbyes seems like eons ago. And as I write these words, I wonder how I did not break down right then and there, from the magnitude and the loneliness of what I had done and was about to do.

It was because the God Who Laughs and the all-powerful Universe who can be kind to its believers also have big hearts.

I am certain of this.

I would rather live my life as if there is a God and die to find out there isn't, than live as if there isn't and to die to find out that there is.
~ Albert Camus

Chapter Seventeen

San Antonio Sojourn

We arrived safe and sound in San Antonio before dark, a modest but welcome ending to a day of intense driving. A curious thing I had noticed along the entire trip was the lack of mask wearing, particularly since the Delta strain had recently surged. It seemed everywhere I stopped or stayed overnight, there were usually only two out of ten people wearing a mask.

Being fearful of getting covid while on the road, I dutifully wore mine whenever I was out of the truck. I was always amazed, though, at the large number of people who didn't, particularly in the Northeast, where people were shunned for not wearing face coverings in public places.

When I pulled into the San Antonio hotel parking lot, and this being Texas, land of mask, vaccination, and covid deniers, I was stunned to see the majority of guests and hotel employees wearing masks.

Knowing it was not mandatory in the state, I was curious as to why, so I asked a young male hotel employee who was wearing one. His reason; he had a newborn at home, and his wife, understandably, demanded that he wear a face covering when at work and around their baby.

What I was seeing in real life did not, in any manner, compute with what I saw on cable news, online news sites, and social

media. Maybe this slice of reality shouldn't have surprised me, but it did.

Several hours prior to arriving at the hotel, and after the frightening downpours outside of Dallas had subsided, the remainder of the drive to San Antonio had become increasingly easy.

And as Mexico became closer, my thoughts naturally drifted to Sharon and our fortuitous meeting two years ago. If it not been for her, I had my doubts whether I would have had the courage to make this significant change in my life, though I'll never know.

Of all the questionable ventures we had confessed to, the missives about the men in our lives were to me the most interesting. To be fair, though, there were both good and bad men to write about, but the stories describing the hair-raising close calls we both had had with unscrupulous men were, by far, the juiciest.

Sharon's close call was a life-threatening situation; she was held hostage for three days by a coke-sniffing boyfriend with a gun. Mine was being sued for everything I owned by a con man I had met online; he went after my business, my house, my cash, literally everything but my dogs.

My demented man had presented himself as an artist, but in actuality he was nothing more than a handsome, miserable con artist who could draw well.

He was the good-looking man I had met before meeting the ugly man from the island who would not humor me by wearing a cowboy hat.

Since I was driving through Texas, the home state of the con man, it was natural that the memory of the immoral creature and the trauma he inflicted upon me would come to mind.

Even though it was a painful, distressing time in my life that was over long ago, it was an experience that I never wanted to forget. But, more than that, I felt it was a significant lesson to share with other women as a cautionary tale of what can go wrong when you ignore red flags.

I eased up on my gas-pedal leg — the numbness was now affecting my right hip — and allowed my body to relax and my mind to roam. I realized, months later, that these mind-wandering expeditions were, among other things, sanity-saving exercises that helped keep worry and insecurity at bay.

Better to be musing over memories from bygone days than to fret over recently done deals or possible future misfortunes that may or may not happen.

Whenever I reflected on the past, most of my memories, except those of men, were of contented, exciting, and fulfilling times. However, it was well into the transition to my new life that these bitter but sweet reminiscences had the ability to make me sad and nostalgic. And, knowing what I know now, I will always be grateful for the postponement of that emotional grieving.

We all mourn the good times, for they are irrevocably and forever behind us, and that is a hard thing for any of us of a certain age to accept.

Truthfully, there are days when I can't help but wonder whether I'll ever have wonderful times like those again. They took years to make, and quantity of years is something I no longer have, not that I ever thought I did.

To make the next few hours of driving bearable — they had truly become boring — I vividly evoked Sharon's and my boyfriend horror-story tales. Though they were shameful and embarrassing, we faithfully adhered to our promise of one hundred percent truth telling.

However, as scary as those episodes were, they also held valuable life lessons for both of us. They were, hands down, worth learning, but only because the harrowing experiences had good endings; bad endings to these affairs would have been devastating, if not deadly.

Lorraine's Con-Artist Artist

Sharon, only for you will I dredge up this horrific story of the man who came close to ruining my life. And after I'm done, I'll once again try to bury these traumatic memories as deep into my subconscious as possible. A task, by the way, I have never succeeded at.

This person, the malevolent antagonist in my story, was, without a doubt, the first truly evil human I had ever personally encountered. My friends and acquaintances who met him briefly or only saw him from a distance did not understand how I could not have seen the malice he emanated. Because love and lust is blind, that's why.

Looking back, I see this experience as though it was a hard-to-believe scoop on an investigative TV show. You know, the shows about seemingly intelligent women being financially taken for a ride by obvious-to-everyone-but-them con men. And as you watch the stories unfold, you cannot understand how these women could have been be so utterly blind, gullible, and stupid. But that, unbelievably, that was my story too.

I was forty-eight, and my biological reproductive stuff had begun to make trouble for me. I had become more indiscriminate in choosing men, and I knew, even at the time, it was a Hail Mary my body was indulging in so that I might have a baby.

While subconsciously looking for a baby-daddy, I heard about online dating, which was in its infancy, and thought I'd give it a try.

It was not very long until I met this monster, and since I was a trusting novice who didn't have a clue about predators on the internet, I was easy prey.

And, Sharon, this is an important side note to my story: I was still drinking like a fish; no excuse, just another relevant detail that I feel sure played a part in my inability to see the truth.

I quickly met twelve men but did not have an ounce of chemistry with any of them. Then I met Mr. Thirteen. He contacted me, and when I saw his photo, as gorgeous as he was, I was immediately disturbed; in fact, I felt repulsed. Subconscious red flags and survival instincts kicked in, but for some reason, I put him into my "saved" folder of possibilities. Months later, I wished I had heeded those flags and instincts and not saved but deleted his profile. I only contacted him after a good friend saw his photo and encouraged me to meet this handsome demon.

He was from Texas but was currently living several hours north of me. It was his idea to come to the island, spend the day, see if we clicked, and take it from there. When he arrived, he was even better-looking in person, and the photographs of his drawings definitely impressed me.

I believed everything he told me, and in no time, I was in love. I had always been a sucker for artistic men with pretty faces. Is there a woman out there who isn't?

We spent three days and three nights getting to know one another — I thought. I showed him all my favorite places around the island in the hope he'd love it too. And since I was smitten and he was an artist, I shared my long-held creative desire to design and produce a line of simple pen-and-ink toile fabrics inspired by my beloved island.

Under my direction, he did numerous single drawings. I would manipulate the drawings and create elaborate toile prints that combined the single drawings in multiple ways.

The verbal deal from the beginning was artwork for room and board, which I honored. Not putting this in writing was a colossal oversight on my part. I had designed fabrics for years and had worked with local artists for trade, but this grifter was not from my island.

After we had lived together for four months, his psychosis began to rear its head. I sincerely became frightened of him the day he waved a knife at me, but I had no way of knowing his craziness was faked in order to scare me enough to kick him out of my house. It was part of his and his pro-bono law firm's calculated scheme for a fraudulent copyright-infringement lawsuit against me.

In the suit, he claimed I had agreed to give him half of my entire twenty-year-old (at the time) business to simply draw objects based on my specifications.

And if he had succeeded in court, he could have taken my house, my money, and possibly everything I had. This unbelievable nightmare, of my own innocent creation, happened simply because I wanted to love and be loved.

Sharon, there are millions of stories like mine, many worse, and certainly not all are women meeting con men stories. I would guess more men, especially older ones, experience this kind of treachery and predatory behavior from women, simply because they have more money to be swindled out of than we do.

Once these new toile designs were printed (I had had them all copyrighted) and shipped to my house and place of business, this man went into frightening rages that lasted for days. I told him to get the hell out and leave or I was calling the police, who knew me and would come to my rescue in a heartbeat.

This entire crazy-town act, Sharon, was part of his plan. His story was: a poor artist with nothing was taken in, used for his talent by a ruthless, selfish businesswoman, and then kicked to the curb without ever being paid a penny.

And I also have to admit to the fact that, during the time we were involved, he had said over and over, "I need to find a good lawsuit so I never have to work again." I just never thought, in a million years, that his lawsuit dream would involve me.

The best medicine to deal with my mental torture was to keep designing my toile fabrics, which would make it clear to anyone who cared that I did not and never did need this devil to be a part of my creative process.

I hired — with a written contract, of course — a local, talented illustrator, and using this new artist's single etchings and my design abilities, I produced a line of beautiful home-furnishing fabrics.

But this time, I promoted my work and received coveted national acclaim. The ole Southern chip on my shoulder once again rose to the challenge. This business move of mine proved to be a wise decision down the road as the eventual lawsuit progressed.

One day, the husband of a couple who shopped in my store every summer came in alone. He told me of their impending divorce; he was living on the island, and would I go to dinner with him? I said yes, mainly because, one, I liked him, and, two, I knew he was a lawyer and I could share my woes with him.

I had not been served with a legal complaint yet, but I knew it was coming. Over dinner, this man assured me that if the worst-case scenario happened, he would be by my side and would help me find the best possible lawyers. He kept his word and saved my home, my career, and possibly my life.

Sure enough, I was served. We sent the complaint to my insurance company, and they quickly denied my claim, but my white knight fought them with beautifully crafted legal letters. On Christmas Eve, I received a letter from the insurance company stating that

they were liable for all my legal and settlement expenses. Merry fucking Christmas is what we both chanted over and over that night as we celebrated with magnums of wine.

We were both alcoholics and suspected as much, but the truth was, we didn't care; it was fun drinking together. He is now also living a sober life, and I'm thrilled for him.

Our relationship didn't make it to the end of the lawsuit, but he had saved me in ways I can never thank him enough for, though actually I did, by being the comfort he needed during his marital woes, which were resolved, and they stayed together in the end.

Just one detail about the mediation trial day that shows how desperate I was to have this nightmare out of my life: it was sometime after 9-11, and the Boston Harbor, like other sensitive areas, was still closed off to all boat traffic except approved ships and barges. The waterways that ran by the federal courthouse where the trial was held were also closed off to most boat traffic.

Before we went into the conference room, I was off by myself, staring at a huge barge traveling up the river, and this is what I thought: dear God, can there please be a bomb on that barge that will blow this building to smithereens.

This, Sharon, this is how much I wanted it all to be over with. I was willing to be dead than live one more torturous day. And the monster, along with his nasty lawyer, would meet their maker, the devil, at the same time.

I'll cut to the end: I won the case, and when it was finally over, I realized the Universe has a twisted sense of humor.

The con artist was number thirteen on the list of men I had met, the letter from the insurance company stating I was to be covered was delivered on Christmas Eve, and the mediation trial date?

April Fool's Day!

Sharon and Her Gun-Toting, Cocaine-Sniffing-Dealing Boyfriend

I was genuinely shocked and taken aback by your story, Lorraine. The deliberate cruelty of that sick man is heartbreaking. And you are right; it is very much like a true-crime drama you would see on television.

Your anxiety levels must have been off the fucking charts, and this may sound terrible, you being sober and all, but it was probably a damn good thing you were still swilling booze back then.

Even non-addictive people would have a hard time not abusing drugs or alcohol through such an ugly, shitty, torment like the one you suffered.

Throughout my own life crises, I have used the World War I mantra — "Just keep on walking, and don't let the bombs hit you." It's in the vein of the A.A. slogan, "One day at a time," don't you think?

There is a small hairy chapter in my life that is similar, but not nearly as consequential, as your torture with Mr. Dating Site Thirteen.

I may have made reference months ago to a man named Daniel, the drug dealer from New York. If not, it doesn't matter. Anyway, here is my sorry, regrettable, and, in the end, life-threatening tale of Daniel, the cocaine lunatic with a gun.

I met Daniel through a friend's friend. I cannot remember what attracted me to him, but I'm going to assume he was the aggressor, because back then,

I slept with anyone who was lavishing attention upon me. Today, I run the other way. These people are suspect, in my opinion.

From the day I met this not attractive but not exactly unattractive man, I was under the impression he had money to burn, which, as it turned out, was what he wanted me to think.

I was so dirt-poor in those days that even my beloved old car was on its last legs. So, naturally, a man with money was appealing, and Daniel seemed like an exciting, rich guy; according to him, he owned a fabulous old rambling house in a tony Manhattan suburb. I bought his whole story, hook, line, and sinker.

Lorraine, you say you were a sucker for artistic men with pretty faces; back then, I was a sucker for horny men with good drugs and lots of money. But more than drugs and money, fun was a requirement, and their usually ill-gotten gains needed to be freely spent on moi, Sharon, the party girl.

Daniel and I must have dated for five or six months when — and this sounds very much like your crazy guy — he began acting bizarre, and I mean life-threatening-scary-bat-shit-crazy bizarre.

I was at his beautiful old rambling house, which, of course, turned out not to be his, when the crap hit the proverbial fan.

I had been staying with my good friend Ed in Manhattan for a few days. Ed knew about my relationship with Daniel and, after meeting him,

called him "colorful." Had he used a more serious adjective — like "dangerous" — I hope I would have listened to him and not the self-indulgence devil murmuring in my ear.

I told Ed I was going out to the suburbs to visit Daniel overnight. I did not have a phone number for his house, and at the time, no one had cell phones, so I was completely unreachable.

Once I arrived at his house, his mood quickly became strange, and when my gut feeling told me to leave, I asked for a ride back to the city.

He left the room and came back with a gun pointed directly at me. I had no idea if it was loaded, but it, sure as shit, was real.

I became his hostage for a full three days that I have absolutely no memory of. And unbeknownst to me, my good friend Ed, along with several other friends back in Manhattan, were panicking over my disappearance. In all the years they had known me, I had never gone missing, not even for a day.

For the life of me, I have no idea how I got out of his house, but I'm guessing he must have passed out from drugs.

There was a public transit strike at the time, which made getting back to the city almost impossible. My plan, though, was to somehow escape, stand on the main road in front of his house, and hitchhike somewhere, anywhere that was a safe distance from this dangerous man.

What happened next was a godsend. I had only been standing by the side of the road for two or three minutes tops, when a nice-looking woman about my age saw me and pulled over.

She asked where I needed to go and why in God's name I was hitchhiking; it was unsafe even in that town. When I blurted out that I was escaping from a crazy man with a gun, she said, "You mean Daniel?" I was shocked when she said this, but hell, I was in front his fucking house, so it was not hard to figure out who I was talking about if you knew him.

Her husband and Daniel had been arrested together for drug trafficking and were most likely going to jail. Once I was in her car, she gave me a terrifying earful — an account of this man I had recklessly wasted my time on for five sex- and drug-fueled months.

I had only a few bucks on me, but this kindhearted angel — and maybe she was just that, an angel — gave me fifty dollars and drove me to a bus station that ran private buses, which were not on strike. If not for her, getting my sorry ass to the city in one piece may never have happened.

Lorraine, okay, what are the odds of me walking out of that crazy house where I had been captive for three days and this woman who knew Daniel driving by within minutes? Astronomical, I'd say.

I never heard another word from him, and I would bet a sizable sum that he is no longer walking this earth; guys like Daniel do not live very long.

Lorraine, my wretched story is definitely a contender for the Most Gullible Woman Alive award, but between the two of us, your story wins, hands down. Wait a second, and not to minimize your potential losses, like your goddamn house, but my losses would have been my life, so maybe I do get the MGWA award!

As I pulled into the hotel parking lot, I looked over at Pearl, happily dozing; in order not to wake her, I quietly exited the truck and checked us in. When I came back, I walked my traveling buddy around the grounds, unloaded what we needed, and straightened Agatha's baseball cap so she wasn't mistaken for a passed-out drunk in the passenger seat.

I wanted her last night as our loyal sentry to be dignified. And since this little vintage mannequin of mine had done a fabulous job guarding our worldly possessions for more than two thousand miles, she deserved it.

Our dear Agatha would soon be disassembled and relegated to the back of the truck with the other mannequins, Clara and Josephine.

I could never have parted with my three custom-made mannequins; they were like old friends to me — beautiful plastic shrines to my former life in fashion. They had dutifully modeled my designs for many years, and leaving them behind was not an option.

The dismantlement of Agatha in the hotel parking lot the next morning was to make room for our new, human passenger, who would accompany us to Laredo. This hilarious mannequin-dismemberment show developed into quite the spectacle for employees and hotel guests who innocently and accidently stumbled upon it.

Once in our room, I fed Pearl the Magnificent, got acquainted with yet another hotel room and its confounding TV remote, then indulged in my favorites: cable news, junk food, a few phone calls, a few emails, and a good night's rest.

"Ahh, heaven," said I, the appreciative, weary old road warrior.

Life must be understood backward. But it must be lived forward.
~ Søren Kierkegaard

Chapter Eighteen

She's Come Undone

Pearl and I did our usual early-morning stroll around the hotel grounds. When we made the rounds, an important sunup chore was to check on our faithful sentry, Agatha. And without fail, whenever I saw her sitting stock-still in the front seat, I instantly broke out in pee-in-your-pants laughter.

The sight never got old for me. It was only a short time ago that this gorgeous, custom-made, vintage mannequin's daily gig was to pose serenely and elegantly in my store window.

And now beautiful Agatha, having no say in the matter, was strapped to a rental truck's passenger seat wearing nothing but a common tee-shirt and a baseball cap.

Understanding my loyal model as well as I did, I knew that, if she could feel, she would be humiliated by her demotion in the world of dummy prominence.

Poor Agatha. But she did have a future in Mexico that she had no knowledge of: being a personal clothes hanger for her boss's clothes. It was unglamorous and involved few admirers, but she would have her mannequin friends, Josephine and Clara, by her side twenty-four seven.

It was not only the memory of her past role in my life compared to the present that amused me; it was also the expression on her face. It was exactly the same whether she was wearing one of my two-thousand-dollar silk organza gowns or a crummy twenty-dollar tee-shirt.

Well, of course it was, but nonetheless, it was damn funny to me. Furthermore, it was damn funny to anyone who walked by and recognized what they were looking at — a gorgeous, lipstick-wearing, baseball-cap-adorned fake human, riding shotgun in a big rental truck.

But today, unfortunately, I had an unhappy Agatha task: taking her apart, limb by limb, hand by hand, along with her lovely head and svelte little plastic torso. And then finding room for these exquisite parts in the back of the jam-packed truck, a job that would not be easy.

When I got over the hilarity of this unusual undertaking that was ahead of me, I realized that the relocation of Agatha was a positive and significant milestone in our trip. It signified that we were nearer to the border, which also meant nearer to San Miguel and our new home.

But, before yesterday, I had given nary a thought to making room for my human friend and former neighbor, who was rendezvousing with us today. It was when I did one of my recurring double-takes of Agatha, perched silently on the opposite side of the seat, next to Pearl, that I became aware of the impending new seating arrangement.

In all seriousness, I said, out load, "Faithful friend, I am sorry to say, to the back of the truck you must go. You did a fantastic job, but it is time for you to join your mannequin buds, Clara and Josephine." She said not a word, just stared ahead, keeping her painted, azure-blue eyes squarely on the road.

Speaking of eyes, among the many pluses of having a live passenger is that a live passenger generally comes with real

working eyeballs that could help me scan the roads for potential dangers.

Also, having two-way conversations with a human — versus the one-way tête-à-têtes I had been having with a dog and a dummy for two thousand miles — would be a welcome improvement, to say the least.

I got Pearl settled in the room, texted my friend for her arrival time, retrieved a moving quilt from the back of the truck, and began my strange and peculiar project in the parking lot.

I stretched the quilt out on the pavement beside the truck, freed Agatha from the passenger seat, and carefully placed her on it. I stripped off her tee-shirt and hat, leaving the poor thing lying naked, faceup, her unblinking eyes staring straight into the harsh Texas sun.

An overweight, middle-aged, midwestern couple innocently wandered by, and as you would expect, they stopped and asked what the heck I was doing.

As I violently yanked Agatha's arms and hands off (she was in desperate need of a WD-40 treatment), I gave the man and woman the short explanation for the bizarre sight before them.

They both nodded their heads the entire time as if it was a perfectly normal and understandable thing to be doing in a hotel parking lot.

In the middle of my tale, I noticed movement in one of the hotel windows overhead. I looked up and saw a man laughing hysterically while giving me a thumbs-up, which I found odd.

But after a few moments, I realized he was probably cheering me on due to a secret desire to do something equally violent and grotesque to his wife.

Every few minutes or so, another hotel guest or employee came by, wanting to know the story behind the naked dummy lying in pieces on the pavement.

Becoming bored with the real story, I began elaborating on it and, within no time, had it morphed into a completely bogus, fun tale of me working with the Texas Rangers.

I told them how I was in San Antonio for a demonstration of how a ranger should manage the situation if he or she came upon body parts on the job — how to wrap them up, preserve them, and so forth.

I also adlibbed about having dozens of dummies in the back of the truck: men, women, boys, girls, fat dummies, skinny dummies, etc.

People will believe anything if you keep a straight face while telling them whatever it is you're telling them.

My friend arrived a few hours later. We spent the evening plotting the next day's drive to Laredo; she caught me up on Vineyard news, and I shared only snippets of my and Pearl's travel adventures.

After all, I had all day tomorrow to tell her the intricacies of outrunning Hurricane Ida, fleeing a car of men I thought wanted to kill me, peeing in gas-station parking lots from New England to Texas, and a slew of other exciting road minutiae.

And for the first time in seven days and several thousand miles, I would have a real person sitting a few feet away with, like I said, ears that heard, eyes that saw, and a mouth that spoke.

But more than that, she was a friend from my former life who had not only supported but witnessed the enormous effort it took to get my new future launched, so no one could have

been a better companion to have in the final hours before Pearl and I crossed the border into a country where I did not speak the language and which I had not visited in years.

> *I tell you, we are here on Earth to fart around,*
> *and don't let anybody tell you different.*
> ~ Kurt Vonnegut

Chapter Nineteen

Last Stop, Laredo

Laredo, Texas, was not the last stop on this road to a new life, but it *was* a distinct demarcation from one journey to the next. No doubt about it.

Mexico's joyful people and gobsmacking beauty, architecture, and culture were another world compared to the one I was leaving. I had been to this remarkable country several times in my life and, on each visit, had developed a deeper respect for its people and their history.

However, my love for Spanish cultures truly began when I lived on Ibiza, an island off the coast of Spain. I remember one afternoon spent poking around the Mediterranean island's ancient fortress, named Old Town; suddenly, and without warning, a premonition took hold of my thoughts, and I knew, as well as I knew the nose on my twenty-four-year-old, suntanned face, that I would live in this culture again.

Now, as I make my way to my new home in Mexico, that premonition from long ago is proving itself true.

As my fellow passenger slept, and due to the sudden memory of the premotion I had in Spain, I was reminded of one of the most favorite times in my life — my unforgettable year in Ibiza, an island known the world over, in the late sixties and seventies, for its exotic atmosphere and wild international hippie lifestyle. It was this time in my life that I chose when Sharon and I asked what years of our lives we would relive, if possible.

Although I didn't know it at the time, this remarkable Spanish island was to become the place where the seedlings for my future career in fashion were to be planted. Also unknown to me, the fruits from those seeds would not fully ripen until years later on another extraordinary island, four thousand miles away.

So with Pearl and my friend dozing, I vividly brought to mind those carefree Ibiza days.

It seemed as if it was only yesterday when I walked that island's volcanic, black-sand Mediterranean beaches and swam in her deep, crystal-blue waters.

Lorraine's Enchanted Year in Spain

You asked me a while ago, Sharon, which time in my life would I relive, if such a thing were possible. The answer was easy — my year in Ibiza, Spain.

What memories to have in my repertoire of life experiences! You told me you had heard of the place, and believe me, if the scene on that hedonistic island was created for anyone, Sharon, it was created for you!

I had sewn my entire life and had made most of my clothing as a teenager; I needed to, because of my unusually long arms and legs. I also created my own style of clothing back then, because the things I wanted and saw in the magazines were not to be found in my little Southern town.

Many years later, that learned ability to sew assisted in my entrée into the fashion world. Because I was able make my own samples, I did not have to hire a sample maker to translate what I saw in my mind's eye into a tangible design to show buyers or even wear myself. Sharon, this sewing skill also came in handy in Spain, and I will tell you why in a minute.

It was around 1974 when I brazenly opened an antique clothing store in a charming old town in Maryland. I was living there with my future husband and needed something interesting to do.

It was brazen of me because I had not a clue as to where the store's inventory would come from. But in no time, through local advertising, I managed to fill the small space with the most gorgeous vintage clothing you have ever seen.

I had set up a workshop in the back of the store and began designing and making my own small line of clothing to fill out the racks. I sewed all day and would have sewn all night if not for my boyfriend, up the street in our little stone cottage, calling and pleading for me to come home.

Flash forward to 1975. For a quite a few years, I had been nursing a severe case of travel lust. It was a restlessness that became stronger by the day.

My good friend in this tiny Maryland town had lived on an island off the coast of Spain; it was also where she had met her French husband. She said, "Lorraine, this is the place for you to begin your wanderlust. It is safe, and loads of interesting hippies from all over the world pass through the island. You will love it." She was right.

Sharon, you were a hippie child from the day you left home. I, on the other hand, did not experience that part of myself until I landed on the shores of Ibiza. What a place to have been when twenty-four and free as a bird. I was free because I had traveled to Spain alone, but I did intend to rendezvous at some point with the boyfriend I had been living with in the States.

However, after I had settled in and began meeting beautiful, long-haired European men dressed in exotic clothing, I could have cared less when that "guy" from Maryland arrived or, more truthfully, didn't arrive.

Within weeks of living on this free-love, international hippie island, my favorite attire became nothing but a printed cotton sarong worn with locally made straw sandals.

And I mean nothing but a sarong — no underwear, no nothing. I wore this big rectangle of thin fabric not just around the house, but on daylong trips to town. I was free in every imaginable way, and sad to say, but true, I'll never, ever be that free again.

Several months into my exciting new Ibizan life, as fate would have it, my American boyfriend did show up. I say American boyfriend because, by this time, I had a beautiful blond Italian boyfriend named Georgio, who also had a beautiful Italian girlfriend named Sofia, but that did not stop us. Up until then, I had never experienced that level of passion in my life, not even close.

At first, I was glad to see my old partner, but I quickly became embarrassed by him. Living in the coolest place on earth and being accompanied by this straight, short-haired, boring-looking American was more than I could handle in my new bohemian life.

But I fixed that style dilemma pronto. I took him clothes shopping at the island's world-renowned outdoor bazaar, Es Cana. Surprisingly, a month later, I was selling not only my own treadle-machine-stitched, handmade clothing there but gobs of cool vintage clothing I had imported from the States.

The Es Cana bazaar was held several miles from town in a beautiful pine forest. Every Wednesday morning, at the crack of dawn, vendors would arrive to claim their pine trees for the day. It was first come, first served.

You know, I don't recall anyone back then having fights over their spots. Hell, we didn't care, we were all just thrilled to be with each other, selling our wares on this exotic, charming island in the middle of the Mediterranean Sea.

My American boyfriend and I made piles and piles of Spanish pesetas but soon realized this currency had much less value outside of Spain. We brainstormed one night and came up with the idea of black-marketing our pesetas for better currencies.

We figured the best place to do this illegal act was in cafés and bars visited by tourists. We would give them better exchange rates than the local banks for their currency; we'd have dollars and deutsche marks, and they'd have more pesetas. It was a win-win, and before long, we had another moneymaking business on our hands.

Being no fool, Sharon, I let my boyfriend do this risky, unlawful business without me. I told him that, if the worst happened, one of us needed to be free and not in jail. He seemed not to mind and, luckily, never got caught.

One of my favorite memories of the island was of an incredible swimming place where giant, flat, sandstone boulders jutted out over the beautiful blue Mediterranean waters.

I cannot remember its name, but dozens of us hippies would gather there on Fridays and have nude picnics. It was fabulous. We were all young, long-haired, and gorgeous, with lithe, naked, suntanned bodies adorned with exotic Moroccan jewelry. We were as internationally vogue as one could get in those carefree 1970s days.

This swimming spot, famous for its beautiful waters, huge boulders, and naked hippies, naturally attracted sightseeing boats, which tooted by several times a day.

To have a little fun, we bare-assed nymphs stood at the edge of the boulders for the tourists to have a closer look. Then, in unison, we'd all turn, bend over, and moon the boatful of shocked and horrified people.

We came to the belief that the tourists did not know what they were in for when they rounded the bend, but the captains of the excursion boats sure the hell did. They wanted their customers to not only get their money's worth from viewing the island's beautiful shoreline but also to have an outrageous naked hippie photo-op and amusing story to tell the folks back home.

My boyfriend/future husband had one of his New York buddies join us on the island for a few weeks. My boyfriend and I mutually decided he should leave Ibiza and go back to the States with his friend. The plan was to take the money we had made at the bazaar and bankroll it into a business he had dreamt of for several years.

Frankly, I was happy to see him go. I had accidently run into Georgio a few days earlier, and not only that, after leaving Spain, I had plans to travel solo through Europe, which I did. I did not want anyone, especially this man, tagging along. It was to be my adventure, and no one else's. And what an adventure it was!

So, yes, I would gladly relive my days in Spain. I have one caveat, though. I absolutely would have to have my twenty-four-year-old body, face, and waist-long, thick, curly, sun-streaked hair. However, and most important, my sixty-eight-year-old brain would get to tag along with that gorgeous, tanned body.

By the way, do I know that I am reliving my past? Look at me, wanting to know what the ground rules are. I am acting as if this is really possible.

Maybe that's because I wish, more than anything, that I could escape this pandemic nightmare.

I'd leave this new terrifying reality in a heartbeat.

Sharon's Secret Peter Pan Wish

Lorraine, you really loosened up a bit in Ibiza, didn't you? I hear today it can be dangerous at night, and the poor island is inundated with loud nightclubs.

Who the fuck knows? I just know I never want to go there and find out. I'll just think of the place as it was in 1976, when you and hundreds of cool, exotic hippies lived there.

Want to hear which era I've always secretly wanted to relive in my life? It's an easy choice — my entire childhood!

I'm serious. I'd like my "relived days" to begin with the first memory I had as a baby and end with the day I left my friends and family and flew to New York.

It was the heartbreaking day when I abandoned everyone and everything I loved to fulfill my dream of becoming a professional dancer.

I had a loving, happy life as a kid. I felt as safe, secure, and protected from the world's problems as any little girl could be. I adored my parents, and they adored me. What more could any kid want?

The reason I end my reliving days on the day I departed from home is that was when life's responsibilities kicked in. Suddenly, I no longer had

my parents' protection from the fucked-upped, unhappy, ill-intentioned people slithering around the planet who thrive and prey on innocent, happy people for the hell of it. A sad, fucking goddamn truth.

Notice my bad language has escalated again. I've been watching way too much Netflix this past week.

Anyway, my friend, my childhood days are the sweet, carefree days that, given the chance, I'd relive in a heartbeat.

My friend is stirring, and Pearl is becoming restless. This amazing dog has been the best traveling companion anyone could ask for. We have grown incredibly close these last few months since we lost our dear Rudy, and I am sure, in the days ahead, we will be even more devoted to each other.

Maybe when we're settled, I'll get us a little Mexican puppy. I feel confident Pearl will be a good mom, and it could be just what we both need to help adjust to our new home and life. (I did just that, and I was right.)

Soon, we three amigas will arrive in Laredo, and my traveling companion/navigator's skills will be called upon to pilot us to the moving company that will unload and store everything until the San Miguel house is ready.

Then, once empty, the obsolete vehicle will be returned to the local truck-rental location. I will miss this comfortable, trusty truck; she was an excellent home away from home, every day, in every possible way.

I glance over and see that my friend's phone screen is on Google Maps. I look back to the long stretch of highway

before us and see the gigantic green road sign hung overhead — Laredo, 20 miles.

Another important milestone that, months ago, seemed far, far away is now upon us. This dream of a new life has never frightened me, but as the miles fly by and we get closer to our new reality down the road, a sense of apprehension flickers around the edges of my consciousness.

And because of this unanticipated moment of uncertainty, I was thankful for the comfort of my companions and felt sure the God Who Laughs realized these momentary feelings of doubt were not planned and so took pity by not making them worse.

I know this to be true, since minutes later, I was my old, spirited, confident self again.

Success is not final, failure is not fatal: It is the courage to continue that counts.
~ Winston Churchill

Chapter Twenty

Banana Stories, Flat Tires, and Not Getting Killed in Laredo

In an earlier chapter, I shared how a number of people reacted to my moving to Mexico. As I get Pearl and myself ready to cross the border, I feel those sentiments and brief conversations are worth mentioning again.

When I first began to tell friends, acquaintances, and strangers I was moving to Mexico, I set into motion a slew of unsolicited opinions, but most of all, over and over, people asked the annoying question "Isn't it dangerous there?"

However, that particular piece of propaganda usually came from strangers, not the people I knew or who knew me. And as time went on and I became more irate over it, I'd lash out with all kinds of comebacks until, after a while, I was able to deal with it by just shaking my head in disgust and walking away.

I've come to believe one of the reasons Americans need to view Mexico as a dangerous country is to help convince themselves that the United States is a safer place to live than it is.

Nothing could be further from the truth, and as more random mass killings happen on a daily basis, the proof of that becomes more and more evident.

Several days ago, when departing Alabama, my friend's husband warned me about the possible dangers in Laredo, Texas — a place, by the way, he had never been.

Once we were off the highway and driving in the actual town of Laredo, we saw nothing that looked dangerous while tooling down the town's commercial strip, nothing like that as we drove around the moving company's commercial district, and, again, nothing of the sort on the way to our beautiful, new hotel for the night. In fact, beginning in Pennsylvania and now throughout Texas, this national hotel chain's Laredo location was the best one of all.

My traveling buddy and I easily found the moving and storage place, their men unloaded our trusty rental truck, and as we were leaving, one of the lady employees kindly offered to follow us to the truck rental drop-off location. After which Pearl, our passenger friend, myself, and two large, heavy duffel bags would then switch to her little station wagon and be dropped off at our hotel.

Luckily, for the entire trip, there had not been one vehicle engine or tire problem — zilch, nada, zip. That is, until we shoehorned ourselves into this nice lady's tiny station wagon. Before I got in, I happened to look down at the right rear tire. It was nearly, if not completely, flat. I could not believe it.

At the very end of an arduous, sometimes worrisome twenty-three hundred miles, this happens?

It was so absurd that it was almost funny. Then it occurred to me: the God Who Laughs was enjoying a last-minute joke at our expense.

I frantically told the lady about her tire, but she simply said, as if it was no big deal, "Get in. Don't worry, there's a gas station *right down the road.*" Since my Alabama friend's husband's warning of danger was still making noise in my head, I kept thinking, if we have a flat tire, we could all be killed on the side of the road by a gang of murderous Laredo men. And then, he and the God Who Laughs would have the last laugh.

Here's something I learned about Texans when I was traveling through their state — everything is *right down the road*. This could literally mean *right down the road*, or it could mean five miles or ten miles *right down the road*. I decided that, because the state is so big, any place within that range is considered *right down the road*.

So, two miles later, *right down the road*, and as I consciously held my breath, hoping to make the car lighter, the gas station finally appeared. Fortunately, their air hose was working, but just as important, the almost flat tire was not shredded to bits and held the air I gave it. My blessed-by-a-priest Saint Christopher medal was at it again.

Not wanting any more surprises, I examined all the car's tires, giving two suspicious-looking ones air. The lady then drove the three of us to our clean, newly built, friendly Laredo hotel. I checked us in, and once inside our lovely, secure hotel room, my friend and I congratulated ourselves on a job well done.

Then we, Pearl included, eagerly collapsed on our luxurious, safe Laredo queen beds with not one single bullet hole in any of us.

Wow, three hours in Laredo, and we were still alive! I couldn't wait to tell my friend's husband how wrong he was.

After a short nap, my traveling buddy, who had rented a car to drive back to San Antonio the next day, decided to go shopping near our hotel. I gave her the priest-blessed medal to take along, just in case.

Before leaving, she asked the hotel desk clerk where the closest shopping mall was. The young woman behind the counter said, "Oh, there's a big one *right down the road* on the left; you can't miss it."

Hours later, my friend returned, loaded down with a variety of computer and phone cords she'd bought at my request. She also, strangely, had an assortment of strawberries, figs, peaches, and, for some reason, two huge — and I mean huge — bunches of bananas.

She told me, "You know the mall the young woman said was *right down the road?* Well, it turned out to be at least six miles *right down the road*, and by mile three, I presumed I was past the point of no return and kept on going."

I asked her what was up with all the bananas. Her explanation for them and the other assorted fruit was actually quite logical. Being on the verge of giving up on the elusive shopping mall, she saw an old man on the side of the road selling fruit and farm vegetables out of his truck. She figured he'd know where the mall was, and at the same time, she could grab some easy-to-eat food for our overnight stay at the hotel.

Little did she know, when she pulled off the road to get directions, that she'd get a forty-five-minute earful of not just this man's life, but a descriptive account of his ancestors' lives in Central America, their migration to Mexico, and their eventual move to Texas.

The highlight of his story, though, involved the hundred-year-old, family-owned Guatemalan banana plantation. As a child, he had worked on the family banana farm before his father lost everything in a four-year drought.

My friend listened to his fascinating story of his family's downfall and his subsequent adventure coming to the U.S. and naturally bought gobs of whatever he was selling. Hence the figs, peaches, strawberries, and over-the-top abundance of bananas, which obviously the old man had not grown in Texas.

He told her he bought and sold them for old time's sake because they reminded him of his carefree, childhood days in Guatemala.

When I asked again, "Okay, but why so many?" she replied that he would not sell the bunches separately; it was buy one entirely overpriced bunch and get another bunch for free. She thought it was easy car food, and since she was driving back to San Antonio early the next morning, she'd take one bunch, and I'd take the other for my morning trip to the border and beyond.

Unfortunately, I told her, you cannot cross the border with any kind of produce. Nevertheless, she seemed happy with her *right down the road* adventure, and it was an interesting Texas tale for her to share with friends back home in New England.

As my friend was relating the Guatemalan man's banana story, I had a difficult time paying attention because I kept remembering another banana tale belonging to Sharon; she referred to it as her Banana Ladies of Wall Street story. And what a tale it was.

I continued to patiently listen to my friend, but as soon as she was finished, I launched into Sharon's unbelievable true story of when she was a young dancer living in the Big Apple. It was so unbelievable that I had Sharon write it down one terrifying day during the pandemic when she thought she may have had covid.

And since, like in all other hotel rooms, the remote could only be operated by a technological genius, our plans of watching a movie were out, and for me, happily, the banana tale was in.

Feeling safe and relaxed now in scary Laredo, I whipped out Sharon's banana story, which I had brought along because I loved it so much.

And so, with great enthusiasm, I began to read the amazing, true account of her Wall Street Banana Ladies days — a truly fantastic tale of nerve and pluck, when she was a naïve, green, nineteen-year-old dancer from the South living an exciting, new life in New York City.

Sharon's Extraordinary
Wall Street Banana Ladies Story

Lorraine, do you remember your wild speculations about what the Wall Street Banana Ladies story could be about? Well, none of them came close to the actual events that took place in the summer of 1971.

I know your imagination is excellent, but even if your guesses — "perhaps it involved the commodities market and the buying and selling of boatloads of Chiquita bananas, or to make some extra money, you ladies farmed your talents out, dressed up as giant bananas, and embarrassed yourselves strolling up and down Wall Street" — were clever . . . well, sorry, my friend, they would not be remotely correct.

And so, as I promised, here is my story of the Banana Ladies of Wall Street!

I had been living in the East Village for three or four months with my friend Sheila and her boyfriend, Paul — the same tiny, Jewish guy with an oversized afro who had organized our May Day trip to Washington, D.C.

Paul was a talented entrepreneur in his own crazy, sometimes illegal way. He was fun, had great drugs, and possessed natural, nonstop energy that attracted everyone who came into his sphere.

He was endlessly thinking of ways to make a buck, and I was usually a willing participant, except when it came to his drug dealing.

Before I knew him, he had made an extended trip to California and returned to New York with an intriguing business idea.

New York City is famous for many things — its theaters, museums, and parks — but among its most charming attractions are its street-food vendors.

These industrious, one-man food gigs began in Lower Manhattan over a hundred years ago and eventually found their way all over the city, especially in busy foot-traffic locations.

In many of the areas people worked in or visited — the Garment Center, Madison Avenue, Wall Street, the South Street Seaport, Lower Manhattan, Central Park — pushcart vendors could be found selling quick, fast food. Most of the fare at the time was of the sandwich, bagel, pretzel, ices, and hot dog variety.

For decades, the vendors who owned these street-food carts were mainly of Italian and Jewish decent. They could be seen carting their tiny restaurants on wheels, every morning and evening, to their designated places, and never did you see a dispute among them as to whose territory was whose — that is, until the scantily clad Banana Ladies showed up early one morning in the summer of 1971.

Paul's brilliant business plan was about to take the Manhattan pushcart scene by storm, because nowhere — and I mean nowhere, Lorraine — were there sexy, young, outrageously dressed, good-looking hippie girls selling phallic food out of little canary-yellow pushcarts.

What my friend Paul had discovered in California were chocolate-covered frozen bananas. They were relatively new on the West Coast but unheard-of on the East Coast. This was soon to change.

It was Paul's idea to introduce these chocolate, dildo-looking treats on a stick to an unsuspecting New York business crowd in a famous, high-foot-traffic area in the city. He figured a busy business area, not a strictly tourist location, would be more shocking, more bang per buck, and would make the biggest splash possible. And Sheila and yours truly were to be the two half-naked women introducing them. It was fucking outrageous, and I loved every minute of it!

The seed of this plan may have been planted in Paul's head in California, but it did not sprout until late one stoned evening in his East Village apartment. He excitedly explained his business idea to Shelia and me, and the two of us were immediately on board. But we were especially excited when he asked us to be the Banana Ladies in his fabulous business venture.

For me, Lorraine, this opportunity could not have come at a better time. I had already made the decision to move to California by the end of the summer and thought this awesome, fun, purely cash job could be the quick moneymaker I needed for my cross-country trip.

Paul's role was figuring out the logistics — where to buy the bananas, pushcarts, etc., but most of all, where to make and store our frozen bananas. He soon found a place a few doors down from our Third Street apartment.

It was a vacant, run-down storefront directly across the street from the infamous Hells Angels' OK Corral headquarters. Paul, who was friendly with the club's members, asked the motorcycle gang to protect our humble storefront, which they happily agreed to; we compensated them with chocolate-covered frozen bananas and marijuana joints. A fabulous combo, by the way.

The Hells Angels guys were great, and I was sure they thought Sheila and I were quite the hot little hippie chicks too, and we were.

During the day, they'd all be hanging out on their motorcycles in front of their headquarters. I'd stroll by and wave, and in my heavily accented Southern voice, I'd say, "Hi, y'all," then pop into our banana-making store to make our frozen foodstuff.

I was never afraid of those tough, scary-looking men, probably because back then, to me, they just looked like Southern, redneck hippies on motorcycles. Which they kind of were.

Besides having the honor of being the first Banana Ladies, Sheila and I got to design and make the outfits for our new exhibitionist-food-cart gig. The biggest fashion trends going that year were hot pants and platform shoes.

I knew how to sew, and Sheila had a sewing machine at her parents' apartment in the Bronx. We spent an entire day whipping up our costumes, while Sheila's parents looked on in horror. They kept saying, "You're wearing that? Please tell us you're not wearing that!"

Our Banana Lady costumes were quite the showstoppers. I made us tiny, bright yellow, satin hot pants and equally tiny brown, backless halter tops.

Amazingly, someone found a couple of extra-large, round, yellow, promotional-type buttons that read "Don't Squeeze My Banana," which we promptly pinned front and center on our flimsy chocolate-brown tops.

It was Paul's brilliant decision that the business area to make our grand debut would be New York's world-famous Financial District.

A few days before the big event, we made a reconnaissance trip downtown and staked out our territory.

I chose the corner of Wall and Broad Streets, knowing nothing about its claim to fame. I just liked the big-time, important look of it.

We had our costumes, our banana-factory store, protectors for said store, orders for bananas set aside every morning at the fruit market in the Bronx, and all the toppings — nuts, chocolate, sprinkles — sourced, bought, and ready to go.

Paul had also managed to find two used, adorable, lady-like freezer pushcarts; they were perfect. I painted them glossy canary-yellow, while on the side of the carts, Sheila drew bad renderings of our frozen, nut-covered, chocolate dildos.

She also unsuccessfully hand-lettered our product's name — Frozen Banana Crunchies — above her "pornographic artwork."

We were still lacking a vehicle big enough to haul the three of us and our two pushcarts around the city to our chosen peddling spots. Paul got wind of government auctions held in Connecticut once a month, and it was there that he bought our fledgling business a used U.S. mail truck.

Early one June morning on Wall and Broad, we introduced our Frozen Banana Crunchies to the world.

Looking back, Lorraine, unbeknownst to me, the hick from Dixie — who donned this outlandish tiny costume and wore her hair so frizzed out it was known to get caught in car doors — was about to have the experience of her life.

At the crack of dawn, we loaded up our Frozen Banana Crunchies truck and headed downtown. Paul dropped me off at my corner. While I was getting my cart set up and ready to go, I noticed people beginning to mill around me. I thought, what the fuck are they looking at?

I had not a clue as to the outrageousness of what I was doing. I was from the South, not New York, and had been under the impression that nothing was sacred or considered weird or strange in this city of freaks and extremists.

People just stood and stared. I thought maybe if I ate one of the things, they would understand what I was doing — so I took a frozen banana out of its wrapper to show what I was selling and how to eat it.

I had the thing in my mouth, and I suddenly realized what I must look like. For a moment I was stunned, but instantly realized that I did not give a shit; I just wanted to sell the fucking things and go to California.

I ate four in a row in front of my stunned audience, and it wasn't very long before I was selling the hell out of my Frozen Banana Crunchies.

The crowd continued to grow, and soon the area I was in, which is much like an open square busy with cars traveling through, was completely jammed with people.

Dozens of onlookers had rushed back to their offices, telling their coworkers about the unbelievable scene down on the street.

Hundreds and hundreds of people piled into their office elevators and came to see for themselves the half-dressed hippie chicks selling chocolate-covered phallic symbols out of yellow pushcarts.

Little did I know that Sheila was experiencing the same thing two blocks away. The event had become a twofer spectacle.

Suddenly, the sea — and it was a sea, of staring, ogling people — began to part, and out rode three cops on horseback. Eventually, they got everyone out of the street, onto the sidewalks, and back into their buildings.

It was wild, and Sheila and I, in our teensy homemade outfits, not the Dow Jones Industrial Average, were the stars on this crazy, fun-filled summer day on Wall Street.

After a few days, the Financial District's Italian vendors began to be a problem. They were out of their minds over their new competition — sexy, young pushcart peddlers — and began demanding that the cops harass us.

The cops, though, loved our scantily clad banana act, but to please the Italians, they would ride up on their horses, lean down, and whisper, "Just move your cart down the street like you're leaving, then move it back when I'm gone."

This went on for a couple of days until the Italians gave up. They knew it was a losing battle because it was obvious Wall Street, including the police, loved their Banana Ladies, and they were not going anywhere.

Every weekday morning for the next three months, we donned our hot-pants hooker outfits with the "Don't Squeeze My Banana" buttons pinned to our chests and went to work on Wall Street, where we too made lots of dough.

Our evenings were devoted to making frozen-chocolate-, nut-covered banana crunchies in our filthy store across the street from the watchful eyes of our buddies, the Hells Angels.

Within several successful weeks of making and selling our crunchies, Paul decided it was time to branch out and sell them in Central Park during weekend concerts. It was a lucrative, no-brainer idea since there would be hundreds of stoned-out hippies who would eat anything when high.

Sheila and I skipped our hot pants outfits and wore our usual tight jeans and tees for those events. Our little pushcarts full of frozen merchandise never lasted more than an hour on those hot summer evenings.

I made money that summer not only for my California road trip but also for the first few weeks of my new West Coast life.

Sheila eventually decided to go on the road with me. We were devoted to Paul and did not want to leave him high and dry, so before we left New York, we trained two new Banana Ladies.

We taught them everything we knew about the selling and making of our now-famous street food.

After we left, Paul and his new ladies made the local New York TV news. Sheila and I were thrilled for them.

Lorraine, that is the story of the Banana Ladies of Wall Street, and every word of it is true.

As I finished telling my traveling buddy the tale of Sharon's Manhattan banana venture and she was giving me a round of applause, Pearl leapt up, barked, and dashed to the door. She needed to pee on more Texas real estate before we left, and being the intelligent dog she is, she also generously left the governor of the state a nice, big, stinky parting gift on the hotel's back lawn, which I of course left there.

Good girl, Pearl. Bad girl, Lorraine.

I was tired from my big day of arrival in Laredo, leaving all my worldly possessions in a run-down storage building and sadly returning our rental home on wheels to its rightful owners. With Pearl squared away, it was time then for us three weary road warriors to call it a night and sleep tight in our safe, cozy Laredo hotel room.

This was my last night in the United States until who knew when. And when I thought about that reality, I knew it was another one I had not allowed myself to think about. Cautiously, I began to allow thoughts about the immediate days ahead of us to float to the surface of my consciousness.

They were only blurred, shadowy images of a foreign culture intermingled with a vague sense of hope. And at this point in my journey to a new life, I'd have to be okay with those visions and feelings, and not let apprehension set in and weaken my resolve.

Even though I was exhausted, I prayed I could sleep, for there were many reasons to lie awake and worry. What if the driver I'd hired to drive me and Pearl through Mexico didn't show up? What if Pearl and I had trouble getting across the border, even though I had crossed every "t" and dotted every "i"? What if the Mexican border officials messed up my visa stamp, which would affect the closing on my house?

What if, what if, what if — the questions didn't seem to matter. I slept like a baby and woke the next morning bright and eager to begin the next chapter of my life.

Mexico, ready or not, here we come.

So we shall let the reader answer this question for himself: who is the happier man, he who has braved the storm of life and lived or he who has stayed securely on shore and merely existed?
~ Hunter S. Thompson

Chapter Twenty-One

Border Anxieties, Checking Boxes,
and Our Duct-Taped Chariot to Paradise

My good friend and passenger left at the crack of dawn for her trip back home, and it was miraculous that I stayed as strong as I did during our goodbyes — she was going home, and I was venturing into the unknown.

Alone.

As I've said before, how I remained resilient and focused throughout this enormous life change is a mystery to me. I have always worn my emotions — anger, love, fear, and passion — on my sleeve.

Years ago, though, possibly because of my business, I learned the advantages of pragmatic thinking. I have no knowledge of how I acquired this ability; I presume it was just a necessity for me in order to ride out bad economic times.

My household belongings are in storage — check that box. My big, black duffel bags are packed with the things Pearl and I will need for a month — check that box.

The two of us, along with our official papers, are ready and waiting for our driver and private chariot to San Miguel — check that box!

While we waited in the lobby, I received a text from our driver saying he would be half an hour late. What I know about this man is this: he is an American, has lived in Mexico for decades, is the owner of the moving and storage company I hired, and his name is Ian.

I also found out from the nice lady who drove us to the hotel that Ian is a bit temperamental (oh, great), and I must pronounce his name correctly. It is *I-an*, not E-an, and on a bad day, *I-an* can be neurotic about the pronunciation of his name.

Damn — a difficult male for nine hours of driving, but there's no other immediate alternative that I know of.

I-an finally texts that he is out front waiting for us. The bellman helps me, Pearl, and our stuffed duffel bags out to the van (the nice lady said it was a van) that will carry us to our long-anticipated new life in Mexico.

As we go through the sliding doors, I see, parked under the hotel entrance canopy, what must be our ride to paradise. I thought, dear God, this dilapidated, rattletrap piece of shit is the vehicle that will take us five hundred miles to San Miguel?

Seriously, as I stood there, trying to grasp the reality of the condition of this van-thing, out popped *I-an*. He ran or (forgive me for this) hobbled around to the sliding-door side of the van, introduced himself, and helped the bellman load our bags.

I instantly knew *I-an* had either been in a terrible accident in the distant past or had had an unfortunate birth defect that severely deformed his right leg. I decided not to ask about his injury; it was up to him to tell me if he wanted to.

Pearl and I got settled in, Ian put our duct-taped chariot to paradise into drive, and off we went!

A few miles down the road, when I asked if this vehicle was going to make the trip to San Miguel, Ian slung his crippled leg up on the console in front of me and said, "Of course, why would you think otherwise?" I then asked when was the last time he had taken a good look under the hood, checked the tires, and so forth?

He confessed the van looked bad but assured me that, mechanically, it was sound. Taking him at his word, I decided to relax — that is, until he told me that, due to a long-haul moving gig, he hadn't slept in thirty-six hours.

I had driven twenty-three hundred miles, had kept Pearl and myself safe, and now this? The God Who Laughs had, unfortunately, not forgotten about us.

Knowing Ian was temperamental and knowing he knew we were at his mercy, which we were, I treaded lightly. It also became obvious that he wanted me to ask about his handicapped leg, but I was sticking to my belief that if he wanted me to know the story behind his injury, it was he, not I, who was going to bring it up.

Later that day, he did. He said, out of the blue, "Don't you want to know about my leg?" I said, "Sure, but only if you want to tell me." He then told the story of his injury, which was caused by a gruesome, tragic childhood accident.

I felt a little kinder toward him after his story, but not enough to squash the burning hostility I had for him. At the last minute, he and his manager had doubled the quoted price for our trip from Laredo to San Miguel.

It was the day before our arrival in Laredo when the manager informed me of this price hike; I had little option but to pay, and he knew it. Anyone would be extremely pissed at this deception of theirs, but I kept my mouth shut.

For the past couple of days, an impending task that had been constantly on my mind was causing me terrible anxiety. I had an important mission with the customs officials at the border.

It was one I could not goof up, which, of course, made it more stressful. Both the Mexican visa page in my passport and my entrance-into-Mexico document had to be perfectly stamped in order to complete the closing on my house.

This vital and serious task was the first thing I thought about upon waking on my last morning in the United States. When I told Ian about this mission of mine, he had not a clue as to what I was talking about.

So, unfortunately, I was completely on my own. And as time has gone by, being on my own in this foreign country has become a fact of life for me.

Ian waited in the van with Pearl in order to keep the air-conditioning running. I had worried about the heat affecting her; she was almost twelve. I mean, hell, we were at the southern border at the end of August, but surprisingly, it was not bad.

The worst heat we had encountered on the entire trip had been in Little Rock, but then again, everything had been worse in Little Rock.

I knew no Spanish at the time, and the customs officials knew no English, but somehow I managed to communicate what I needed.

I was utterly shaken, though, when one of the three officials frowned after entering my passport number into their ancient-looking government computer.

He said, "*Uno momento,*" then walked down the hall to another room. I was privately freaking out; the man had my damn passport, and what was it on his computer screen that caused the look of concern on his face?

It worked out in the end. "It" being a bullshit game border officials sometimes played just to mess with people's heads. Well, that's the conclusion I came to anyway.

I knew all along that, if need be, I could enlist Ian's help. He spoke fluent Spanish and crossed the border on a weekly basis; plus I had paid him more than enough for a few "extras."

I managed on my own and, once finished, went outside to where Pearl patiently waited in our pitiful, duct-taped, dilapidated, but air-conditioned chariot to paradise.

Per instructions from my real estate agent, I photographed, then texted the stamped visa papers to her. She was anxiously waiting in San Miguel for these documents so she could continue with the paperwork for the closing on our house. I got a thumbs-up text and, without thinking, let out a deep sigh of relief.

The months of anticipation for this very important moment had been executed perfectly, and I could now stop fretting and forget about it.

Another box checked, celebrated with a big kiss on Pearl's snout.

I began quietly accepting this crappy van we were fated to travel in. And by dropping my snooty American attitude, I started to embrace this embarrassing vehicle that had long ago lost its shock absorbers.

I realized that it was probably better to drive through this particular stretch of highway looking like hard-working Mexicans than fancy Americans.

My blessed-by-a-priest Saint Christopher medal was at it again, and maybe, just maybe, ole *I-an* knew precisely what he was doing.

The real voyage of discovery consists not in seeking new landscapes, but in having new eyes.
~ Marcel Proust

Chapter Twenty-Two

Ian the Terrible

After the ordeal with the customs officials, I climbed back in the van with my pal Pearl and told Ian we were good to go. As a precaution, he decided we should have the vehicle, along with my bags, inspected before hitting the road.

He said it wasn't mandatory; we could just hop back on the highway, but his instincts said we should go through the border inspection. I figured he knew what he was doing, though he could have been testing me to see if I had contraband packed in my bags. He didn't know a thing about me; I could have God only knows what in my duffel bags, and if we had been stopped and inspected by the *federales* and they found something — well, our lives as we knew them would have taken a sharp turn for the worse.

We pulled into a parking lot adjacent to the customs office, and three young men searched the van and my bags. What I found odd was that they did not search our persons, nor did they give Pearl a second glance.

I'd been told that if a dog looks ill, they'll ask for veterinarian papers and give the animal the once-over. But she was obviously healthy-looking, so we passed with flying colors and found our way back to the highway.

Ian once again slung his injured right leg up on the console, put the pedal to the metal, whipped out his phone, and began to text.

I watched in horror for about thirty seconds, then firmly told him to immediately slow down and put his phone away. I was relieved when he did exactly that. There was no way on God's green earth that I was going to go one more kilometer with this reckless lunatic if he didn't honor and respect my and Pearl's lives, much less his own. He quietly uttered, "Yea, my wife hates my texting while driving too." I said, "Well, duh, *Eeee-an,* it's a dangerous combination, don't you think?"

With that confrontation out of the way, I settled back into the van's lumpy bench seat, pulled Pearl close, and struck up a friendly conversation with him. I had concluded that one reason Ian may have doubled the price for our ride to San Miguel was that he was not in the mood to drive nine hours with some Yankee lady and her fancy poodle; he was going to make putting up with a rookie gringo and her yappy dog worth his while.

Boy, was he proven wrong after about an hour of my storytelling, and me being my congenial self and Pearl being her fabulous doggie self.

He also soon began to appreciate the fact that he and I were both just old hippies, living unconventional lives, and my move to Mexico was a continuation of my preference for an alternative lifestyle.

I honestly sensed a little remorse on his part. He realized he had ripped off a nice old hippie like himself and felt bad (I think). But there was no way he was going to refund me half my money, so I took pleasure in his guilt. I also felt more comfortable knowing he wasn't a totally unempathetic jerk.

We had been driving for an hour or so when, suddenly, we slowed to a crawl that quickly became a complete standstill. Ian got out his phone and looked at our position on Google Maps.

This is the deal, he said: we can stay on this highway for the next ten kilometers, but it will be bumper-to-bumper because of roadwork. Or we can go through that town you see over there on the right. Going through town would take at least an hour. I told him it was his call, and he chose to stay on the highway. What did I know? Nothing.

Thirty minutes later, we had barely gone half a kilometer, Ian looked at Google Maps again, and angrily said, "Oh fuck! Fuck me! I was looking at the map upside down." At the time, I thought, is that even possible, but since there was no turning back to take the alternate route through town, we were stuck with the course Ian had chosen. My only concern was, did we have enough gas for the ten kilometers of bumper-to-bumper driving? He said we did, so what could I do? Nothing.

Unbeknownst to me, though, in just a few minutes, the fun, wild ride through half of Mexico was about to begin.

Almost all the vehicles on the highway were big eighteen-wheelers loaded to the gills. In fact, I don't remember any cars. I think our old ramshackle van was the only non–big rig on the road at the time.

Ian had obviously been in the same situation on this very road, because he knew how to get around the trucks and speed things up. There was a bumpy, extremely potholed dirt road running parallel and a little downhill from the highway.

Suddenly, Ian shouted, "Hold on!" He whipped the wheel to his right, veering off the paved road, and aimed the van down the small hill onto the bumpy, rutted dirt road.

We must have been going thirty-five miles an hour in our shock-absorber-less heap. It was so much like riding a bucking broncho (I imagined) that I'd holler out, "Ride 'em, cowboy" every time we'd go over an extra big bump. Pearl got into the swing of things too, giving big barks when her mama did her shout-outs.

Whenever we pulled off the paved highway, which we did five or six times, we could travel only about a kilometer or so before the road temporarily ended. This was due to big drainage ditches cutting perpendicular into the alternate side road. When Ian came to these deep trenches, he'd swing the van back up the incline to the paved highway.

The truck drivers did not like our creative traffic dodging one bit and would swerve their trucks toward us every time we attempted to get back on the road. But Ian knew how to expertly squeeze our dilapidated chariot right between their big rigs, no problem.

This crazy ride went on for ten kilometers, and I have to say I loved every minute of it. But, truthfully, I thought every big bump could be our last. And so, not to worry too much, I would hold Pearl close each time and say to her, "Pearlie, what do you think of Mexico so far?"

A loving lick in my face was always her answer.

Buy the ticket, take the ride.
~ Hunter S. Thompson

Chapter Twenty-Three

*Matehuala Pit Stop and
the Jetson Time-Travel Motel*

After the ride-'em-cowboy traffic adventure, and four hours into our nine-hour trip, Ian informed me that he could not complete the drive in one day. His thirty-six-hour, nonstop driving gig prior to picking us up in Laredo had caught up with him.

When he saw I was upset with the news, he said there was a small town two hours down the highway named Matehuala where lots of travelers stayed on their way to San Miguel. And now that he knew I was a lady up for fun and adventure, he made the pit stop more enticing — we would stay at a very cool, old motel from the 1960s. He described the place as a time warp; the owners over the years apparently had never updated or changed anything except the sheets, towels, bedspreads, and televisions. This turned out to be absolutely true.

It was an easy-off, easy-on place right on the side of the road, and to placate me even more, he made the unscheduled overnight stay, including dinner, his treat.

I had already paid for a penthouse apartment rental for four nights in San Miguel, but if he was footing the bill, sure, let's stay at the Jetson Time-Travel Motel, courtesy of Ian the Terrible.

In the meantime, and not long after the traffic jam, the landscape began to dramatically change. This was the very beginning of September, the last month of Mexico's rainy season, so the vistas were green and lush.

The altitude also began to change; I could feel it in my ears as they began to pop — yawn-pop, yawn-pop, yawn-pop for forty-five minutes as our rusty heap made the long climb up the mountain.

I was absolutely astounded by what I saw out the van's filthy windows (Ian cleaned them when we stopped for gas). The views were breathtaking. I had not a clue as to what the Mexican landscape would look like. I had been so caught up in my get-there-itis, I had not given a thought to the country's terrain from Laredo to our new home.

The old van had begun to grow on me as it passed every challenge thrown at it: potholes, ruts, reckless drivers cutting us off, high altitude, you name it. And it had another, highly prized quality — it was invisible; no one noticed us. We blended right in with all the Mexican workers driving their beat-up old vehicles. Yes, I have to admit, ole Ian knew what he was doing.

With Pearl cuddled by my side, I sat back, relaxed, and let my mind wander while enjoying the scenery out our now clean, shiny windows. Suddenly, out of the blue, like many of my mental wanderings while on the road, and for no reason at all, the calm, vista-filled views of the Mexican terrain prompted another road-trip memory from my days while living abroad.

This peculiar tale took place while I rode with American friends on a Spanish bus from Alicante to Granada to visit the Alambra. The couple in this story had just visited my future husband and me in Ibiza, Spain. It was a spur-of-the-moment whirlwind trip I will never forget.

Lorraine's Strange
Bus Ride to Granada, Spain

Sharon, I loved your wild story about driving across country, especially the part where your fellow road tripper, Lori, fucked one of your Oklahoma-hippie hitchhikers in the back of your van. Even more hilarious was how you and she tried to ditch them at the next gas station because of her embarrassing indiscretion, but they refused to get out of the vehicle, knowing what you would do if they did!

Here's my reciprocating road tale of a curious and weird bus ride I had while living in Spain. I was still living in Ibiza with my boyfriend when an American couple we had met in Jamaica paid us a visit.

The husband, Joel, was an architect, and the wife, Carol, an artist. Besides their constant nagging for a little sexual partner swapping, which I always refused, the four of us had a wonderful time on the island together.

They loved going to the weekly Es Cana bazaar with us; Joel took amazing photos of the array of international hippies, while Carol helped me hawk my vintage clothing and handmade shirts sewn on my treadle machine in our country finca.

The day our friends left, as we drove them to the boat that sailed from Ibiza Town to the Spanish port of Alicante, Joel told us that, after landing there, they were going to fulfill a yearslong dream of seeing the Alhambra in Granada.

At the time, I had never heard of this ancient Moorish castle, but while driving to the boat and hearing about its history, I became more and more intrigued.

I clearly remember turning to my boyfriend and saying, "Do you have your passport and money with you?" His answer being yes, I

replied, "Well, me too. Let's hop the boat and go to the Alhambra with them." He looked startled for a moment, thought about it, and realized there was nothing stopping us but us. So off we went!

We had money to buy whatever we might need for this spur-of-the-moment adventure, and I was wearing a pair of long pants and a real top — not my usual sarong with no underwear — so fashion-wise, I felt comfortable with our impulsive trip to Granada.

It was a four-hour boat trip to the mainland, and then an arduous, seven-hour bus ride down to Granada, where the Alhambra waited for us to explore her magnificent architecture.

Sharon, I remember nothing about the boat ride to Alicante, and neither does Joel, whom I spoke with last night to see what he remembered of our strange trip to Granada.

The boat landed in Alicante in the late afternoon, which was a blessing, as the four of us were like lost children in the woods. I can't imagine us getting there in the black of night or even finding our way out of a paper bag. None of us spoke a lick of Spanish, which was not necessary in Ibiza, where nearly everyone spoke a little English.

Somehow, though, we fumbled our way to the bus station and bought tickets to Granada; unfortunately, the bus didn't leave until one in the morning.

"One in the morning?" we all said. Then, "Shit!" we all said. We were bummed, but since we had hours to kill, we agreed to fool around in town and have dinner somewhere near the bus station.

A funny memory I have of our dinner that evening centers around the waiter and his bizarre smile, which Dracula would have been envious of. Joel loved taking photos of the Spanish people, so when

the waiter walked up to our table, introduced himself, then gave us a big, ear-to-ear smile, Joel immediately whipped out his camera. But the waiter clamped his lips shut, never to smile for him again. Maybe you had to be there, Sharon, but at the time, it was hilarious.

Joel tried everything, but the waiter would not, no matter what, crack a smile that showed his teeth. However, he did bring his entire family out from the kitchen to have their pictures taken.

The nonsmiling father, who was elegant in his white shirt, black pants, and waist-to-floor white apron, stood proudly in the center of the family lineup.

I still have that photo (I took one too) of the family with big smiles across their faces, except the father, of course; even he knew how shocking his vampire teeth were. It was cruel of us, I know, but at the moment, we just wanted a photo to remember him by.

After dinner, we went back to the bus station and boarded the bus to the Alhambra. It was pitch-black once we left the small port town. This was 1976, mind you; today it's probably a sprawling city with lights stretching miles out of town.

We could see nothing but blackness out the windows besides whatever the bus headlights lit up — I mean, absolutely nothing — which seemed strange to us.

Carol and my boyfriend were sound asleep within minutes of the bus's departure from the station. Joel and I foolishly had had espressos after dinner and did not sleep a wink the entire night except for an hour or so before daylight.

Unbeknownst to us, Mother Nature had a glorious surprise for everyone on board when the sun rose the next morning in her cloudless blue sky.

The bus rolled along, stopping every once in a while for a passenger standing in the dark alongside the road. What became

nightmarish outside our windows, besides the total blackness, were the strange, deserted-looking villages, one after another.

The bus headlights made shadows on the charcoal-gray buildings. They looked like dark, dusty stucco ghost towns; not a single light from a house or a glow from a street lamp could be seen anywhere.

This peculiar and actually creepy scene went on for hours. Joel and I decided we had accidently entered the Twilight Zone, and we were never going to escape; we'd just ride this old bus in the black of night for eternity.

In the middle of this strange, disturbing bus ride, Carol woke up, could not find her passport, and freaked out. I mean, really freaked out, like shouting, "Oh, my God, oh my God, my passport is missing!" while running up and down the aisle of the bus.

It was like a bizarre scene out of a film noir; everything had a dark, twisted quality to it. She was so hysterical that the driver pulled the bus to the side of the road.

The four of us had changed seats early on, and that is where Carol eventually found her passport, wedged between the cushions of her original seat. We were so relieved because she kept frantically saying we had to get off the bus and head back to the Alicante bus station. Which is exactly what we would have done had she not found it.

With that drama out of the way, she and everyone on the bus went back to sleep, except of course, Joel and me, the espresso-wired, night-terror duo.

For several hours, we continued to be amazed and simultaneously horrified by the show outside our windows, until, thankfully, we were put out of our misery and fell fast asleep.

I was exhausted and sleeping like a baby when I felt a tug on my shirtsleeve. It was Joel whispering, "Lorraine, wake up, and look

out the window." I opened one eye and was so flabbergasted at what I saw, the other eye flew open, and I instinctively smashed my face against the glass for a better view.

Stretched before us, as far as one could see, were thousands of acres of seven-foot-tall sunflowers, all standing proud and ripe for the picking. I have never forgotten that amazing sight and never will. Our bus experience went from a nightmarish quality to one of awe-inspiring beauty — a golden, glorious, morning sun, shining its rays down on hundreds of thousands of giant sunflowers.

Every bus window was filled with this magnificent sight; no matter where you looked, sunflowers were everywhere. It reminded me of swimming off the coast of Mexico years ago, when I encountered a huge school of fish. I dove into the middle of the school and opened my eyes, and no matter where I looked, there were identical fish looking back at me, hundreds of them — above me, below me, to the sides of me.

Sharon, that huge school of fish was an incredible, remarkable sight, but not a beautiful and joyful one like seeing the thousands and thousands of sunflowers surrounding our little Spanish bus bound for the Alhambra.

That, my friend, was just one of my many road-trip stories. I, like most travelers, also have train- and plane-trip tales, but I'll save them for another time.

My mind may have wandered back to Spain, but my present vision was filled with the breathtaking Mexican landscape outside our windows.

Ian was keeping the old van at a good clip as it made its way down the highway, bringing us closer and closer to our overnight stay at the Jetson Time-Travel Motel.

It wasn't long before I saw a fabulous old sixties motel sign on a long pole, high in the sky, and sure enough, I had the impression we were tumbling back in time. It was not just the motel and its classic, towering sign; it was the highway and the businesses alongside it that also had a vintage sixties quality to them.

I turned to Pearl and told her there was possibly a handsome dog named Astro at the motel. I mean, this place really looked like there might be an Astro dog living there and a George and a Judy working the front desk. I couldn't wait to see what the rooms looked like, and they did not disappoint — total sixties décor.

I took loads of photos because the existence of this place from another era was hard to believe. And in this case, Jetson Time-Travel Motel pictures were, without question, worth thousands of words.

Pearl loved the grounds, open spaces with palm trees and cacti where she could run free, something she had not been able to do on our long trip.

We both were happy, especially me, knowing that San Miguel was now only a day's drive down the road and the closing on our new home less than a week away.

After we got settled in our blast-from-the-past motel room, I fed Pearl and cleaned up for dinner. I could not wait to see what was on the motel's restaurant menu.

Would it be chicken ala king, fondue, or vegetables encased in green Jello? It was none of these, but what it was I don't remember because it was so bad; I was glad Ian was picking up the check, since I would have sent it all back.

It was time for bed, and time to check in with friends back home. I hoped, more than anything, that I'd get a decent

night's sleep on the lumpy, bumpy, who-knows-how-old mattress, that, thank goodness, had nice, clean 2021 sheets on it.

After all, tomorrow isn't just another day. It's the first day of our new life in San Miguel.

Holding on is believing that there's only a past; letting go is knowing that there's a future.
~ Daphne Rose Kingma

Chapter Twenty-Four

Adios, Matehuala,
Hola, San Miguel!

I woke at the crack of dawn, looked around my motel room, and thought, where in God's name am I? It took a few seconds, but I then remembered — oh, right, the Jetson Motel in Matehuala, Mexico.

This was the first time during the entire trip that I had awakened and wondered where I was. I roused Pearl and took her for a walk on the motel grounds and thought about how wonderful it will be where we are going, a place with few or no ticks — what a relief!

I had just had my fifth bout of Lyme disease before leaving, and poor Pearl had had two herself. Regardless, I will miss my old island home, and all the ticks in the world cannot change the forty-one years of unconditional love I have had for the place.

As I was admiring my elegant dog prancing in big circles on the motel lawn, Ian came stumbling out of his room, stood beside me, and watched the magnificent Pearl in all her glory.

He said he had been so tired, he had barely gotten a wink of sleep. This made me nervous, especially since I didn't know what the drive ahead was like. Was it straightforward or occasionally dangerous, like yesterday?

I had driven over two thousand miles with *my* hands on the steering wheel, and letting go and allowing *Ian's* hands to be in control had not been easy for me. But there was not much I could do other than make sure he did not speed or text while driving.

And pray — yes, I could pray and kiss my blessed-by-a-priest Saint Christopher's medal a few dozen times during the final stretch to San Miguel.

After a quick breakfast, we hit the road mid-morning under a glorious, blue, sanguine Mexican sky.

The highway, which seemed flat, in reality was thousands of feet in elevation, and so I kept the yawn-pop, yawn pop going to adjust my ears to the altitude pressure.

Since Ian's driving and actually Ian himself were subdued in comparison to the day before, I let myself once again become captivated by the gorgeous terrain outside our windows.

While observing the little businesses alongside the road here and there, I was struck by the thought that this country and its culture, which is completely foreign to my home county, may very well be where I will spend the remainder of my life.

I had thought about many things, mostly logistical challenges, in the last several years; however, I knew that, whatever my next life chapter's circumstances were to be, good or bad, they must be experienced, not guessed at or imagined.

And so I never sweated the inevitable moment when it all became real, with real consequences, not romanticized scenarios in which I could control the winds of fate to suit my needs and fantasies.

I relaxed knowing we were only hours from our final destination — *final destination*, scary but welcome words to me. I suddenly, but not surprisingly, began to contemplate my former life. Thinking about my past with abandon was a risky diversion I had not yet allowed myself the freedom to do.

That life was behind me, and the one ahead had no guarantees, only faint whiffs of possibilities. I had little power over the consequences of my recent past actions at this juncture. I had seriously needed and wanted a new life and was about to get my wish. And yes, on some days, the refrain *Be careful what you wish for, Lorraine* played over and over in my head.

I leaned back in the torn, old bench seat and let the memories and images of my beloved island life surface and wander where they might. And if I became quiet and pensive, Ian would either notice or not notice. Much like this old rattletrap, the man had grown on me, and he could be just the guy to unload on.

I presumed he had driven lots of women and their dogs to San Miguel — women like me, making new beginnings, who may have had last-minute moments of apprehension and fears of possibly having messed up their lives forever. As it turned out, I never needed his shoulder to unburden myself on and was glad, not knowing how he may have reacted.

One reason I had not allowed my mind to drift to my past was because my favorite memories were those of my dogs. Whenever I envisioned the island, its trails and beaches, the images and remembrances of my four-legged friends were there, and I just could not bear the bittersweetness of those visions.

Although I did think, since we were nearly to San Miguel, maybe reminiscing would not be such a risky thing for me to do; the excitement of being this close to our new home might drown out any sorrows and uncertainties floating around in my subconscious.

So, with trepidation, I allowed myself to remember bygone days in those last few hours before we reached our journey's end and a place I would soon call home.

I was all of twenty-eight when I discovered the incredible island of Martha's Vineyard off the coast of Massachusetts. I had left my husband (the boyfriend in Ibiza) and sold our Manhattan loft in reaction to what I still, and always will, refer to as an epiphany.

That significant and extraordinary event occurred on one of the island's pristine ocean beaches, and to this day, I remember exactly where it took place.

The message was clear and strong — Lorraine, this is where you will live, this is where you will thrive. And so, I gambled my marriage, my business, and my future on that vision.

My marriage did not survive.

Our glorious island was a safe, warm cocoon for myself and my peers. Together, on that patch of land in the Atlantic, we grew to adulthood and beyond. And, without a doubt, for all those years, we considered ourselves the luckiest people in the world.

The parties, the music, the days on the beaches, sailing to neighboring islands, businesses we opened, artistic endeavors we supported, the marriages and raising of families — those were the most extraordinary times, ones that we, collectively, will never forget.

Beautiful memories, like our beautiful island, will always be part of our personal histories and forever in our hearts and minds.

Now, in this unfamiliar and uncertain moment in my life, looking back, I know that, at the time, we were the most fortunate people in the world. And we still are for having lived those unforgettable years in one of earth's most spectacular places.

In my mind's eye, I saw the many friends and lovers I'd known, the beautiful antique cars I'd driven on the island's small, winding roads, the charming homes I had lived in, the loyal customers whose faces I can never forget, the thousands of garments I created, and the stories that went with them — on and on, my visualizations went, bright, fleeting flashes of a wonderful life well-lived.

These quiet pangs of homesickness that I experienced while being tossed around in the back of our rust-bucket chariot brought to mind one of Sharon's more heartfelt tales.

It was the sad-but-brave story of leaving her Southern hometown a month after graduating from high school. She left her family, childhood friends, actually everything she had ever known in her life for a dance career in Manhattan, a place where she literally knew no one.

As I get closer to my future, this saga of hers hits home like no other story she told. And the reason is obvious — I am making a similar unproven move at sixty-nine, just as she did at a mere, inexperienced eighteen.

Sharon's dream, fueled by pure naivety mixed with ambition, was the drive behind her life change. *Unlike* me, though, she never looked back with the kind of love and longing that I seemed to be facing.

She was young, possessing a spirit so filled with wonder and curiosity that it softened the pain of loss, but also, *like* me, she had not a smidgen of security ahead of her.

Sharon, though, had two parents who were still alive, and this particular circumstance, unlike mine, provided a soft place, emotionally and physically, for her to land if her dance plans failed.

I had been orphaned and divorced for decades, so I was without any kind of safety net if my efforts ended in failure. I did have my experienced older self and a few good friends I could count on. And in a worst-case scenario, that would have to do.

In these last hours, as the ole van chugged successfully up another mountain and nearer to our final destination, I affectionately thought back to Sharon's story of courage and loss.

Sharon's Brave Tale of Courage

Lorraine, I hope this narrative, in which ignorance played a big part, helps you in your gigantic, humongous, enormous, frightening, risky, and perilous move to a new life in a foreign country that you basically know nothing about.

Ha ha ha ha. Seriously, though, I am your biggest supporter and fan in your brave decision to make a new life for yourself. And don't you ever forget that, basically, it was my idea, remember?

Therefore, I will assume responsibility in the event it blows the fuck up, and together, we can go live somewhere under a bridge of your choosing.

With those depressing thoughts out of the way, and since today, another Fourth of July holiday, is

honoring and celebrating our country's independence, I want to share the fearless but painful day of my own independence at age eighteen.

I may have alluded to that time in my life, and though I've told you a shitload of fucking crazy stories about my past, I don't recall telling you about the day I left everything and everyone I loved for the dream of becoming a professional dancer.

This is not another outrageous story, Lorraine. This was a pivotal and serious moment in my life and one I would never change, if given the chance. It was, though, without a doubt, the most difficult decision I have ever made.

I had thought my memory of this day was clear, but years later, when my best friend from high school showed me a photograph, the depth of my sadness became real.

In the photo were a half dozen or so teenage girls sitting around a fountain outside the airport, all there to say their goodbyes to me.

Not a single face wore a smile, and the expression on my poor little face was so forlorn that, even many years later, it was heart-wrenching to look at.

I wanted to comfort that young girl; she was so brave and innocent as to what lay ahead of her. She only knew the tiny world of her Southern town, the one she'd grown up in, where nothing bad had ever really touched her or her childhood friends.

Yes, this is the green, naïve me I'm writing about, Lorraine, not the sassy, fuck-you-world Sharon that I became.

Don't you find sometimes, when you look back on your life, it's as if you're two people, one young, trusting, courageous, and a little crazy, and one older, pragmatic, wise, still adventurous, but cautious from the traumatic experiences life threw at you?

I don't know about you, but I am still and always will be these two people; one individual never eclipsed the other.

I remember getting on that plane to New York City full of optimism, hope, and excitement. I don't recall being nervous, sad, or afraid, except that, based on that photo I saw years later, clearly I was.

At that age, life feels forever — not like now, when I know that the years I have left, whatever they may be, are precious and few.

After I had moved to New York, I would often return to my hometown, unconsciously juicing up on the familiarity and love I was missing in my now big-city life.

However, I was slowly being weaned from that small-town security; the pull from the past was being vanquished by the pull from the future, and that is how I kept moving forward, one new experience at a time.

And that, Lorraine, is the story of what it was like to leave the only world I knew and the people I

loved in it. It was left behind for unknown adventures, good or bad, and is very much like what you are about to do by leaving your much-loved island home.

But I will be here for you. I always have been.

Because of the musings of my past and my head in the clouds remembering Sharon's valiant story, the remaining hours to San Miguel flew by, and it was not until Pearl uncharacteristically barked at nothing that I realized we were there.

Were we *there,* or were we *here?*

There or *here,* it didn't matter. The road adventure had just come to its long-anticipated, inevitable end. Processing this significant moment, wrapping my head around it, took some time — hours, days, weeks, and, truthfully, months.

Once we were in town, Ian drove our heroic, dilapidated chariot to the rented penthouse apartment where we would spend our first few days.

He had wanted to leave us at the moving place he owned, but I nixed that idea immediately, reminding him how much I had paid him. The house manager for the town house met Pearl and me on the street and gallantly carried our bags up to our gorgeous digs with a view.

The first thing I did, wherever we stayed, was feed my faithful road companion. This chore told her that this was home — or, more to the point, another place that catered to her desire for top-quality chicken parts.

Man, what a dog! She was there for me twenty-four/eight, and her devotion and good-natured behavior never wavered. I only

wished, as we crossed the Mexico border, that she had left more stinky presents of eliminated poultry for Texas's shitty governor.

I unpacked a bit, then, with my gorgeous wing-girl Pearl by my side, went out to explore the beautiful town of San Miguel and her cobblestoned streets of intrigue and promise.

It's never too late to become who you want to be. I hope you live a life that you're proud of, and if you find that you're not, I hope you have the strength to start over.
~ F. Scott Fitzgerald

Chapter Twenty-Five

Our New Home,
San Miguel

Pearl and I had a peaceful first night in our new hometown of San Miguel. However, there were moments, throughout the night, when I had to remind myself — Lorraine, you are no longer a traveler on that long road to your new home. Nor are you and Pearl driving wildly through the mountains of Mexico in Ian's rickety old van.

At daybreak, I dashed out to the terrace and gazed for the umpteenth time at our spectacular view. It was a foggy, misty morning, and I could see very little, but slowly, out of the mist, a beautiful hot-air balloon emerged, then another and another.

And as the three balloons drifted low over the celebrated little town, the Parroquia's bells at the top of the hill began to chime.

Having no idea of the time or the reason for the church bells, I said to Pearl, "Pearlie, look — San Miguel is saying welcome, welcome to your new home." She cocked her head, barked, and trotted to the door saying, "That's great, Mom, but I need to pee!"

I got dressed, walked Pearl around the block, then made our way to the gorgeous, flower-filled park we had discovered the evening before. I grabbed some coffee for myself, a few treats for Pearl, and headed back to the apartment.

Once there, I checked in with the realtor for our Mexican house, who was of course, relieved that we had finally arrived safe and sound in San Miguel.

For this new life to begin, many things, not just our road journey, had to fall perfectly into place, and amazingly, they all did.

The God Who Laughs must take naps now and then.

Since it had gotten fairly hot outside, I decided to leave Pearl in the apartment while I poked around town. To be truthful, I was searching for the antiques shop where I had met Sharon nearly two years ago.

I will never forget that day; it was one that, for many years, I had longed and hoped for. Even though those years had brought much happiness, joy, sorrow, and loss, I had sadly begun to think my adventurous spirit over the years had faded and was never again to be the shiny beacon that had guided me during my youth.

But I also wondered, could this trait have been simply a creation of my youthful, wanderlust-filled self? And if that were true, when did I, someone who had never played it safe in life, become so pragmatic, focused, ambitious, and, quite honestly, boring?

Perhaps, though, and more to the point, was my boringness simply due to my being bored?

On my prior trip to San Miguel, I had spent most days discovering the town, wandering alone down her winding, cobblestone streets without worry or concern. My mind was filled with memories of the younger, passionate, daredevil me, who decades ago had also walked alone down narrow cobblestone streets in a similar Spanish town thousands of miles away.

Where, oh where, did that courageous, inquisitive woman go? And are bravery, confidence, and curiosity also casualties of old age?

The day I saw Sharon's reflection in that gilded mirror was the day I understood that passion and spirited wonder, like love, do not always wither and die; their fires can burn bright forever.

In that moment, when my eyes met my own dark, girlish eyes in the mirror, I knew my venturesome self was still alive and my neophyte lust for adventure, and all that it entails, had been given a second chance.

> *Fateful encounters like this are the ones we all dream of, and they are usually just that — dreams. But this was not a dream; this was real. While admiring a beautiful, ornate gilded mirror, I caught the reflection of an eerily familiar young woman. I became fascinated with her when, suddenly, her dark eyes locked on mine.*

That encounter — the ethereal woman of long ago metamorphically meeting the contemporary woman of today — ignited a profound life transformation, and there was no turning back.

It was the amalgamation of young woman and old woman on my reconnaissance trip in 2019 that brought me back to this remarkable country and inspired this long-awaited day:

I was alone, sitting with strangers around an elegant, antique table. However, I was not entirely alone: Pearl was nestled at my feet, the sole connection to my former life. And the feeling of this beloved dog's warm body against my leg was the only reassurance I needed for any doubts I might have in this life-altering moment.

The people in this small room — two realtors, two lawyers, and a translator — were here to witness the signing of formal papers making the home I had bought from afar officially mine.

This meeting was the culmination of two years of diligent and, at times, overwhelming work — all of it done during the waxing and waning of a global pandemic the world had not seen in a hundred years.

The interpreter carefully explained in English what each page meant, and when instructed, I signed and initialed the lines required. Until this house closing in Mexico, it had been years since I had signed my full name so many times at one sitting.

As the pages were read aloud and I was asked if I understood, I would nod yes. Then, when directed, I would scrawl my two given names — *Sharon Lorraine* — before my surname.

Over and over, I signed *Sharon Lorraine*, and it was the same at the bank the next day. I soon learned that my full name was my official name in Mexico, where, incredibly, every "t" was crossed and every "i" meticulously dotted. Actually, the more names before your surname, the better. A four- or five-name signature is not uncommon in this country.

After the closing on the house, a huge sigh of relief escaped my still road-weary mind and body. A grateful hug of thanks to my Mexican realtor was in order before I loaded myself, Pearl, and our bags into her car.

Next up, a quick stop at the *tienda* for a few days' supply of food, and off we went to the house I knew only from a thousand, dreamy, online glimpses.

I asked the realtor to please just drop us off in front of the house; she need not come in. Not surprisingly, she understood — I wanted to be alone with Pearl as we walked together for the first time through the entrance to our new home.

And so, with great fanfare and a bit of struggle, I carried my canine companion over our Mexican casa's threshold like a beautiful bride, dressed from nose to tail in pure white.

Once inside the house, I tenderly put Pearl down, got on my knees, held her face in my hands, looked in her eyes, and thanked her for being my wing-girl and loyal companion for the nearly three-thousand, sometimes nerve-racking miles we had traveled. It was her safety alone that kept my thoughts clear and focused on the task at hand, including the job of having enough chicken and cookies for her wherever we stopped.

We went from room to room, me opening cabinets doors and closets and she sniffing and inspecting the nooks and crannies, hoping to discover uninvited critters she could chase away. Then out to the luscious, plant-filled courtyard, where Pearl, who had never encountered a pool before, promptly fell in.

Once she was rescued, we snuggled together on the outdoor chaise lounge. As we dried off in the warm Mexican sun, I took in our new home's surroundings. The palm trees, birds of paradise, and bougainvillea were ours, really ours.

This awe-inspiring environment — chock-full of butterflies, hummingbirds, and exotic birds whose songs I had never heard — left me mesmerized and full of wonder. All I wanted to do, or really could do, was be still and observant.

While a tired, contented Pearl slept in my lap, I called upon the Universe for a favor — a grace period, a much-needed honeymoon from the crazy, complicated world outside the vine-covered courtyard walls we now called home.

I had long been a participant in the divided world of right and wrong, good versus evil, generosity overshadowed by greed, and intelligence insulted by ignorance.

My hard work and relatively benevolent footprint on this earth for nearly seventy years had earned me a respite from the day-to-day challenges, if only for a brief while.

In the cool, early evening, I leashed up Pearl the Magnificent and dauntlessly set out to discover this new world of ours. Its bright blue skies, bountiful beauty, potential friends and foes, its countless unknowns and infinite possibilities were all out there to become part of or, perhaps, not part of our lives.

And, as I would soon find out, paradise is a fragile, fleeting frame of mind, and staying positive in the face of profound human flaws, frailties, and negativities would take more strength and courage than I ever could have imagined.

Be kind, for everyone you meet is fighting a hard battle
.~ Plato

You know it never has been easy
Whether you do or you do not resign
Whether you travel the breadth of extremities
Or stick to some straighter line.
~ Joni Mitchell

Epilogue

This Much I Do Know

It has been more than two years since Pearl and I arrived in San Miguel. And unbeknownst to us, the day we drove into town, the newest member of our family, Ruby, was being born.

Making this coincidence even more remarkable, our little puppy came into the world only a few blocks from our new home. However, finding her before anyone else did (by pure chance, I found her online) was the real coup de chance.

While Pearl had never been fond of other dogs, except her uncle Rudy, she immediately became a doting mother to baby Ruby. And not only did this amazing canine become Ruby's protector, she quickly grew into a dog who no longer perceived other dogs as a threat.

She began to see them as possible friends, although, if they messed with her puppy, watch out! More than once, I saw firsthand the instantaneous transformation from congenial dog to ferocious mama. It was quite scary and, at the same time, an amazing thing to behold.

After a year and a half, Pearl, Ruby, and I adopted — our response to an unavoidable dilemma for dog lovers in San Miguel — two fabulous neighborhood street dogs, Mike and Molly, (aka the M&M's).

And since taking in these grateful critters, on many occasions, while writing at my desk, I've stopped, looked around, seen my four loyal companions sprawled on the floor, and said, "Hey, Lorraine, what's to complain about?"

Well, let me tell you!

The much-needed and well-earned grace period I requested from the Universe, that first day in our new house, when I cuddled with Pearl in the Mexican sun, came and went far too fast.

The reprieve from conflict and the Universe's blessing of the temporary serenity I had prayed for lasted a mere four months, then — wham, reality set in.

If I had consulted a bona-fide soothsayer in advance of my move and they had given me a preview of the first two years of my new life, it would have been difficult for me to have believed. And knowing myself for seventy-plus years now, a clairvoyant's vision in no way would have changed my decision to go forward with this transformative move.

I knew, from the moment I decided to uproot my long-established life and exchange it for a new one in a foreign land, that this new life and whatever idiosyncrasies and future relationships it held could not be preplanned or understood beforehand. Instead, it would have to be *lived*. Not guessed at or wished for, but *lived*.

And, if anything had ever given me pause, it was one big, troubling uncertainty — what if the unknown and all that it entailed were to become too much for me?

All of my other concerns were just logistical questions, with answers out there somewhere. It was only a matter of me finding them.

Why Are We Like This?

I was grateful that my first couple of months in San Miguel were uneventful, but as more time passed, the unfolding of this new reality became something I had never experienced before.

I wish *blossoming*, not unfolding, was the more accurate word, and perhaps someday, when I look back at this time, it will be.

The simple truth is this: when I had made radical moves earlier in life, it was a kinder, gentler world, and I was a much younger woman.

And, interestingly, my logical mind never considered the way in which politics, along with the pandemic, has affected society, especially people's behaviors toward one another.

This terrible but true fact, in my opinion, is staggering, though none of us should be surprised by it in today's world — saddened by it, yes, but not surprised.

Even now, as I write these words, there are very few weeks that go by when I am not taken aback by some unkind word I hear or rude manner I see or experience, and to be honest, it is rarely a Mexican I notice behaving badly.

I am convinced that the root cause of this awful, shameful behavior I have been exposed to is an extreme level of unhappiness.

And the fact is that this delightful town of San Miguel did not make anyone this way.

These unhappy people, who came from who knows where, are the same disgruntled humans as they were before they arrived in Mexico.

I don't get it.

Growing Pains

There have been days when I've thought I was alone in living through this kind of hurt and confusion, and why not? I had never been seventy years old, living friendless in a foreign country.

But as I unburdened my troubles with trusted friends from my past, I came to realize that I share this particular experience with millions of older, hardworking, often successful men and women.

People like me, who, at the appropriate time in their lives, give up their professional identities can and do experience years of sometimes profound personal crises. And it doesn't make a difference if you stay where you are or if you move five hundred or five thousand miles away. Nor do the circumstances when you get there matter; surrendering a lifelong identity is traumatic, especially for those who loved their work and loved it passionately.

As I attempt to understand and survive this moment in life, I know the path to acceptance can sometimes be in how you frame a difficult situation. Explaining the traumas I've experienced so far as *growing pains* has put my mind into a more positive, progressive, and open place.

I remember when I stumbled on the practice of reframing. It was with my first poodles, Noli and Cleo, during one of our evening drives to the beach. In my beach-going days, those two crazy, wonderful dogs were always wild and out of control in the back seat of the vintage Volvo I drove in the summers.

I would scream at them to knock it off and stop being so fucking obnoxious. Did they listen to me? Of course not, and as a result, the day came when I realized that it was going to be up to me to change, dog training be damned!

So, from then on, I thought of their crazy behavior in the back seat as simply out-of-control enthusiasm, which it was, and nothing more.

And because of that day thirty years ago and the invaluable lesson from those two fabulous poodles, today I am able to interpret these trials and tribulations as unfortunate, but necessary growing pains.

My Charming Casa!

Many people in San Miguel choose to rent, even live in different neighborhoods for a while before making the commitment of buying a house. From the beginning, though, I wanted a home of my own, and so I bought one and have absolutely no regrets.

By owning a house, I have had the great privilege of getting to know Mexican laborers and their hardworking attitudes. If I had limitless funds, I would buy and rehab houses for the sheer joy of being surrounded by these joyful, playful men day after day.

It is not only the workmen I adore; it is equally the absolutely beautiful, mind-blowing stonework, tiles, and carved wooden objects they use in their work. I will forever be amazed and inspired by this beauty. I have never seen this kind of craftmanship in my life. It is truly astounding.

Watching the tradesmen construct houses, additions, and walls out of piles of concrete and sand, sometimes mixed directly on the cobblestone street in front of the building site, is a vision to behold.

Observing their strong, suntanned hands taking earthen materials and turning them into incredible structures right before your eyes is an experience you cannot forget.

If there is anything I am sure of after these two years, it is this: I am, without a doubt, blessed to live among and become familiar with the Mexican people, their history, and their culture.

And So?

Have the disappointments and stresses that I have endured since my arrival here been worth it?

Have they been outweighed by the intermittent joys, the power of the beauty that surrounds me, my home, and the companionship of my four amazing dogs?

For now, and possibly just for now, that is a question I cannot answer.

But this much I do know: I will happily live, though perhaps not forever, in this beautiful, charming town of San Miguel de Allende, unless, once again,

Adventure rears its beautiful head.

About the Author

Lorraine Parish has been a well-known East Coast fashion designer for forty-four years. In 1979, she relocated her downtown Manhattan business to the beautiful island of Martha's Vineyard.

In the summer of 1980, she opened her first Vineyard store in the rural town of Chilmark. There her designs caught the eye of the island's celebrity crowd: Carly Simon, the Taylor clan, Rose Stryon, Mary Steenburgen, the Cronkite family, established political figures, and many summer Hollywood notables.

She began publishing national catalogs in 1986, which inspired the openings of Lorraine Parish stores in Aspen, Colorado, Boston, Massachusetts, and Nantucket,

Massachusetts. In 2001, she launched Lorraine Parish Home, her signature line of modern toile fabrics and home furnishings.

Feeling restless as she approached a major life milestone and sensing it was time for a new chapter in her life, she took a trip in 2019 to the celebrated Mexican town of San Miguel de Allende. In this charming locale she fell in love with the Mexican people, their country, and their culture.

As her love of writing grew and the pandemic began winding down in 2021, she gave up her fashion career, sold her Vineyard home, bought a casa in San Miguel, and began fullfilling her love of writing essays, screenplays, and now her first book, *Miles to San Miguel*.

*The most profound smack of reality you can face
is the realization that most of your life is behind you.
I wish you strength and peace when you experience yours.*
~ Lorraine Parish

Made in the USA
Coppell, TX
18 November 2023

24422569R00118